Capricorn

The Ultimate Guide to an Amazing Zodiac Sign in Astrology

Your Free Gift (only available for a limited time)

Thanks for getting this book! If you want to learn more about various spirituality topics, then join Mari Silva's community and get a free guided meditation MP3 for awakening your third eye. This guided meditation mp3 is designed to open and strengthen ones third eye so you can experience a higher state of consciousness. Simply visit the link below the image to get started.

https://spiritualityspot.com/meditation

Contents

Introduction

The stars and planets have always played a significant role in our lives, and this has been true since the beginning of time. Each of us is born with our own destiny, with no exceptions. Even though we are each just a small part of the universe, we have our own cosmic significance.

In ancient times, there were a lot of stories or myths created around such things. They gave the stars and the planets a lot of importance. Stars and planets acted as a guide and divinity for people. While there are a lot of skeptics now, there are also many believers. There are also those who are curious and want to learn more. Whatever the reason may be, astrological and astronomical factors are an inescapable part of the world.

When we are born, we have a certain blueprint created uniquely for us. It is a combination of genetics and characteristics related to the astrological time at which we are born. The extent and exact details can never be predicted, but the horoscope is something that people have looked to for centuries. We find a lot of information about our destinies and ourselves through our sun signs.

One of the earliest mentions of the zodiac is found in Babylonian astrology. Their concept was further influenced later by Hellenistic culture. It is believed that the sun signs represent many characteristics of the people they are related to.

This is why people have always been interested in learning about the zodiac; it helps them learn about themselves and the surrounding people. In this book, we will focus specifically on one particular sign in the zodiac – Capricorn. You will learn about the traits unique to people belonging to the sign of the Sea-goat. This book will reveal the secrets behind the mind and heart of a Capricorn at every stage in their lives.

You will understand what their strengths and weaknesses are, along with what they seek in life. While each individual on Earth is unique in their own way, learning about their zodiac signs can help us learn about them. So whether or not you are a Capricorn or if your friend, spouse, family, co-worker, or child is one, this book can be immensely useful as a guide to figuring out this sign.

The ancient art of astrology has been regaining popularity over recent years. Learning about your zodiac sign and horoscope can act as a reference point in your life. It will give you guidance and more valuable insight.

A broad range of topics has been covered, from Capricorn as a child and adult to Capricorn's compatibility with other signs in love or at work. Being in tune with your zodiac sign or learning about the Capricorn in your life will increase the potential of leading a happier life.

As you read this book, remember to keep an open mind. This will help you discover a lot about Capricorns as well as the other zodiac signs.

Chapter One: An Introduction to the Capricorn

Capricorn is the last earth sign among the twelve zodiac signs. It is also considered one of the cardinal signs and is a negative earth sign. The ruling planet of this house is Saturn, and the origin is from the horned goat constellation of Capricornus.

You have probably seen it being represented by a goat figure when you check your horoscope or read about zodiacs anywhere. This symbol is a sea-goat, a mythological creature with the tail of a fish and a goat's upper body. There is also a relation to Enki, who was the god of wisdom and water for Sumerians. In the mythology of Babylonians and Akkadians, he was later called Ea and was considered the god of intelligence, magic, creation, and water. The equivalent of Capricorn in Hindu mythology is Makara, and the crocodile represents the sign.

- Date: If you are born between December 22 and January 19, you are a Capricorn.

- Symbol: The sea-goat.

- Element: The element is Earth.

- Polarity: Negative.

- Ruling house: Tenth.

- Quality: Cardinal.

- Tarot card: The Devil.

- Favorable Colors: Brown, Khaki, Black, and Purple.

- Colors to avoid: Yellow and Red.

- Famous Capricorn celebrities: Michelle Obama, Kate Middleton, Liam Hemsworth, Dolly Parton, Diane Sawyer, Kit Harington, Denzel Washington.

Symbolism and Myths Associated with Capricorn

The mythology associated with the sea-goat representing Capricorn can be traced back to the Bronze Age. For the Babylonians, Ea was a protective god of creation, water, and knowledge. The sea goat also has other associations in Greek mythology. It is linked to Amalthea, the goat that nursed Zeus when he escaped his father's wrath as a baby. Another tale depicts how the broken horn of Amalthea became Cornucopia. Cornucopia was the horn filled with earthly bounties.

This zodiac sign is also linked to Pricus, who was the father of sea goats. Pricus tried to protect the sea goats by turning back time when they wandered onto dry land and lost their ability to think and speak, but he had to give his children up to the wild. Pricus then made the constellation of Capricorn and gained an immortal home in heaven. Pricus' tale is considered the reason why the melancholic and sad stereotype is associated with most Capricorns.

Season

The season of Capricorn begins on 21 December in the western zodiac. This is when the winter solstice starts in the northern hemisphere. The light and heat from the sun are at their lowest during this time of the year. The length of the night is somewhat greater than that of the day. From the winter solstice, the days start a slow ascent towards the spring equinox as they lengthen. The spring equinox will represent the last and fourth season of the year. The activities of a winter mirror the affinity of a Capricorn for preparedness and resourcefulness. Conservation and hibernation take place for most creatures in this season.

Mode

Capricorn is one of the cardinal signs in the zodiac. It holds the elemental energy of leadership and initiation. The beginning of winter marks the Capricorn season when energy and light levels are at their highest. The root of the strong cardinal authority of a Capricorn and their nature is the season's definitive quality.

Element

The element associated with Capricorn is earth. It is the most solid and heavy element. Ancient astrologers considered the earth to be the densest form of all matter. This element represents everything that nature is built of and upon. Without it, there is nothing that could take material form. The affinity of a Capricorn to lead, administrate, and wield material power are all linked to the earth element and its tangibility.

Planetary Rulership

Domicile of Saturn: According to classical astrology, Capricorn and Aquarius were both ruled by the planet Saturn. They considered Capricorn the nocturnal resident of this planet. This disciplined and ambitious earth sign allows the expression and enactment of Saturn's most authoritative and stern functions. Being organizational, productive, and practical are all abilities thus granted to a Capricorn.

If you are born with Saturn in Capricorn, these abilities will usually come naturally to you. Such folks tend to have an innate sense of responsibility and duty. They use it to bring order and structure to their world. Capricorns are born with a deep sense of awareness of any adversity around them. They also accept that they were built to weather the hard times they would encounter.

The Detriment of the Moon

This zodiac is in polarity with Cancer, which is a cardinal water sign. Since the moon rules Cancer, people of this sign are emotionally nurturing, protective, and sensitive. They are comfortable being vulnerable and innately intuitive. This contrasts with Capricorn folks, who are a lot more serious.

Capricorns have a stronger work ethic and want to achieve more so others acknowledge them. The moon in Saturn compensates for this detriment. Someone born in this placement tends to have a protective barrier around them and their emotions. It takes a Capricorn a long time to open up to someone completely and show vulnerability. There can be a Saturnian effect due to this placement and cause these natives to have bouts of depression or sadness.

If they are wounded emotionally, they are prone to become cynical. Such experiences make it difficult for a Capricorn to trust people again. Folks with the moon in Capricorn take a long time to admit a need for emotional support. They always pride themselves on their self-reliance and independence instead.

Exaltation of Mars

Mars is the planet of war, drive, and combat. It has a specially exalted place in the sign of Capricorn. Mars's power and propulsion will blend uniquely with the single-minded and steady work ethic of a Capricorn. This placement allows the creation of people good at martial arts and other sports. They also have strategic and tactical minds.

Such people work towards their goals helped by their strengths and endurance in an orderly manner. This placement helps to subdue the rash qualities of Mars and allows its energy to be stabilized so its natives can persevere and endure well.

Fall of Jupiter

According to classical astrologers, Jupiter was exalted in Cancer, and there he expressed his knowledge, benevolence, and expansion in an auspicious way, but some say that Jupiter had his fall in Capricorn, which is the opposite sign. A detriment is more of an adaptive challenge compared to this, but it still causes discomfort to the planetary force.

Capricorn is an earth sign that is cool and dry. The archetype is reserved and cautious, while Jupiter promotes optimism and faith. This is why the energy of Jupiter cannot flow freely. Instead, natives develop cautious optimism where they find it difficult to believe that the universe is working in their favor or that they have good fortune. But Jupiter's enthusiastic qualities may still shine through and allow these natives to survive the adversities they face in life.

House Rulership

Tenth House

The Twelve Letter Alphabet is a modern astrology system. Here, every zodiac sign rules a certain house amongst the twelve in the birth chart. Psychological astrologers created this innovation to help match the related house topics to the sign affinities. The tenth house of career and public status was assigned to the Capricorn zodiac. This happened due to the ambitious and earthy pursuits of a Capricorn that align with the tenth house's concerns. Time and patience tend to rule Capricorn, which is why Saturn's analytical sub-signature is invited to this house.

Twelfth House

According to traditional astrology, Saturn is the planetary ruler of Capricorn. Some say that the twelfth house is where Saturn finds its joy. The twelfth house is one of confinement, isolation, and solitude in the birth chart. Classical astrologers also called this house the house of a bad spirit. This meant that the twelfth house was connected to themes of anxiety and shadows which can cause mental anguish.

It is this relation to Saturn which is responsible for the biggest trials and tests that a person faces. It manifests as a feeling of being burdened with many concerns and responsibilities. This is why Saturn is better able to express itself in the twelfth house, but this placement can be considered good despite its difficulties because it is also linked to the theme of persevering until the defeat of all hurdles.

Characteristics of a Capricorn

Personality

The personality traits of people in this zodiac are derived from yin qualities that are receptive and feminine. This is why Capricorns are engaged with their inner awareness and oriented towards contemplation. Regardless of gender, a Capricorn will be disciplined, determined, and masterful. This is at the core of a Capricorn man or woman's personality. It displays their resourcefulness and resilience in the face of the cold season they are born in.

Capricorn is a cardinal zodiac sign and thus has the qualities of a builder, climber, and achiever. They can set lofty goals and achieve them by taking one step at a time. People born with this sign are reliable, consistent, and determined. You can also see them often deliver a lot more than they promised. Those with the sign of the sea-goat take their reputation and honor a lot more seriously than others.

Chapter Two: Capricorn Cusp Profiles

While learning about a Capricorn's characteristics, you also need to consider those who come into the cusp category. A cusp is when a person's birthday falls right between two zodiac dates. You are considered as on a cusp if you are born within the three days before or after the transition from one zodiac to the other. For Capricorns, there are two such cusp profiles.

One is the Capricorn and Aquarius cusp, while the other is the Capricorn and Sagittarius cusp. The first is at the end of the Capricorn period, while the other is at the beginning of the Capricorn period. Such people tend to have characteristics from both of the houses they fall on the cusp of. This is why inner conflict is a real issue in their personalities. Such people have difficulty making decisions because their different traits are always clashing with each other. As you read more about the two Capricorn cusp profiles, you will better understand this.

The Capricorn-Aquarius Cusp

If you were born between January 17 and January 23, then you were born on the Capricorn-Aquarius cusp. A person born in the Capricorn-Aquarius cusp tends to possess polarized and contrasting energies, making them unique individuals. You tend to be a hardworking idealist, and in the tarot world, you are considered an amalgamation of the Cusp of Mystery and Imagination.

If you look at the two signs separately, they differ greatly from each other. Yet, this combination allows these individuals to look at the world with an unconventional perspective in unparalleled ways. The ruling planet of Capricorn is Saturn, also known as the planet of lessons and limitations. This encourages Capricorns to have a very practical outlook on life and focus on their real-world responsibilities.

But the Aquarius sign's ruling planet is Uranus, which pushes people to develop radical and unconventional thoughts and gives them the ability to open the minds of people around them. When these two stark personalities come together, it can create a powerfully brilliant, creative, and ambitious individual.

Since the Capricorn-Aquarius cusp is a contrast of personalities and perspectives, which are the elements capable of influence, you can also create a complex contradiction as well. The Capricorn side, or the *earth* side, is extremely grounded and determined, while the Aquarius side, the *air* side, has a strong affection for spontaneity and variety. This can be a challenge considering that you have to feed both these halves of your personality, but if you can channel these energies in a healthy and productive fashion, you can grow and succeed no matter what life may throw your way.

A person born on the Cusp of Imagination and Mystery tends to have a lot of internal excitement. You may find your mind constantly churning out interesting thoughts and creative ideas, and you have a chance of experiencing more epiphanies and breakthrough moments than most people, but this constant output of dreams and ambitions flowing through your psyche can make you seem uninterested and detached from most people and situations you might be in.

A person born on the Capricorn-Aquarius cusp can stimulate conversations, making them look like a wiz while conversing with other people. You can see the world for what it really is, and you are drawn to discuss its problems and find ways to fix it. While this gives you the ability to have intriguing and fascinating conversations, it can be isolating and intimidating when it comes to connecting with your close ones, such as your friends and family.

Your mind is teeming with wisdom and unconventional opinions about different issues pertaining to you and the world, but this might keep you from checking on your friends and family, and it can lead to estrangement and strain your personal relationships. Although it may be a very noble endeavor to think about the bigger picture, you should not forget to take a breather now and then and check on your loved ones and nurture your personal relationships.

If you are born on the Capricorn-Aquarius cusp, you can be certain that your life will not be dull. While you are not grinding and working tirelessly on your creative ideas as well as the social connections you have, you are filling your life with excitement and purpose. As a unique individual, you can become a powerful leader and inspire meaningful changes if you will put effort into it, but be mindful that even the most profound ideas need the support of the surrounding people; do not neglect to put effort into connecting with the people in your life and making them feel appreciated.

Strengths

Self-determination, creativity, wit, empathy, and idealistic thought processes are just a few of the many strengths that people on the Capricorn cusp possess. Being born on the Capricorn-Aquarius cusp, you are naturally blessed with a strong drive for success and creativity while formulating your thoughts.

Although these contrasting character traits might clash, these differences allow you to envision meaningful and positive changes and have bigger ambitions and ideas. You can empathize with others and put yourself in their shoes, allowing you to look at the world from different perspectives. This makes you a great friend and a kind and generous soul, if you take the time to have conversations and listen.

Weaknesses

When they aren't at their best, detachment, chaos, selfishness, critical thinking, and prejudice are the vices common with the Capricorn-Aquarius cusp. Because you have to be so involved with creativity and imagination to keep yourself motivated and busy, you may inadvertently close yourself off in your own world, and you may feel like you do not need the company of other people to add meaning to your life.

You become more comfortable being alone with your own thoughts, and this can unintentionally leave your loved ones feeling unloved and unappreciated. This can become counterproductive and have a negative impact on your personal relationships, which is a shame because these people also happen to be some of your greatest supporters.

Suppose you are born on the Capricorn-Aquarius cusp. In that case, you need to remember the importance of a strong support system and put effort into your personal relationships now and then, or they may become a hindrance and affect you in negative ways.

Compatibility

If you are born on the Capricorn-Aquarius cusp, freedom and self-sufficiency are extremely important to you. You tend to thrive on your own, and more than often, you may feel like commitment and codependent relationships are not your cup of tea, but you also require the support and companionship that a lover has to offer. It may take time before you settle into the idea of having a partner, but once you do, you will find that a good companion helps to keep life fun and light.

Fire signs tend to be more compatible with the Capricorn-Aquarius cusp; they will be drawn to your creativity and your work ethic, and they readily offer their support and easily get behind your unconventional and radical ideas. Air signs such as Aquarius, Libra, and Gemini also make good companions for the Capricorn-Aquarius cusp. They can keep up with you intellectually and understand your not-so-emotional personality better than the other signs.

Key Takeaways

Develop the habit of self-assessing and reflecting on your emotions sometimes. Although it may be easy to get lost in your own head and keep yourself occupied, you also need to keep yourself grounded and keep one foot in the real world. You do not want to miss out on the small but meaningful conversations happening around you.

Try to listen to others while they are talking to you and keep your prejudices and preconceptions in check. Everyone cannot be as quick and creative as you are. If you maintain self-awareness and put in the effort, don't forget to enjoy your life and have fun; this will keep the sense of possibilities and imagination alive for you in the long run.

The Sagittarius-Capricorn Cusp

People born between December 18 and December 24 are a part of the Sagittarius-Capricorn cusp. You will become a true visionary, and you have a capacity for tremendous success. The Sagittarius-Capricorn cusp is also known as the Cusp of Prophecy, and your inherently strong willpower and determination will help you achieve anything that you set your mind to.

Jupiter, as the planet of expansion, rules Sagittarius, while Saturn, as the planet of limits and lessons, rules Capricorn. This means that you have the best of both since they are not so contrasting as compared to the Capricorn-Aquarius cusp. This unique combination of sensibility and inspiration gives you the ability to be not only a great visionary but also a practical realist who can inspire real changes.

As a Sagittarius-Capricorn cusp, you are fueled with a strong passion characteristic of a Fire sign (Sagittarius) as well as the strong willpower and determination of an Earth sign (Capricorn). This helps you make your way through life with a fierce tenacity that most people lack. Your fire sign helps you stay positive and excited to face life, but that alone can die out quickly if not supplemented by the consistency and willpower of the Earth element. Learning to balance these two elements of your personality can help you achieve a lot more than you might think.

People born on the Sagittarius-Capricorn cusp tend to be loyal, caring, and socially active. People who love and admire them and have a genuine interest in the things they have to say constantly surround them. Being reasonable and enlightened as you might be, people will constantly turn to you for advice and support, and you will find yourself providing guidance to the people that are a part of your life. Just remember to be empathetic and gentler to the people who come to you looking for advice. You can be a powerful leader and teacher to those who need it as long as you are patient and don't get aggressive with people; after all, not everyone learns at the same pace.

The concoction that is the Sagittarius-Capricorn cusp can create brave and hardworking individuals who are ready to grind and put in the work that success demands. You will be a motivated individual who is eager to climb the hierarchy and create your own meaningful space in society, but this strong drive and focus can create a rift between you and the people around you if you let it go unchecked. Your uncompromising attitude and independent personality have the potential to change the world, but it might also leave you feeling a little lonely now and then.

Being born on the Cusp of Prophecy, you will have all the potential right at your disposal. While you should be grateful and humble for this natural energy and determination within you, you need to channel it and let it out through positive outlets. You have the potential to make a genuine difference for others as long as you have a definitive plan. If you can be empathetic towards others and have a fun journey to the top, you will become the great teacher and leader that you were destined to be.

Strengths

Those born on the Sagittarius-Capricorn cusp are responsible individuals with a strong drive for success. You also have the ability to be outgoing and friendly towards other people because of your fair and humorous nature. Your strong desire to expand your knowledge allows you to experience and learn from everything that life has to offer.

When this is coupled with your fiery drive and undying determination, it can give you the ability to create a positive impact in your life as well as on those who are a part of your circle. You can delve deep into complex ideas while also being organized enough to pave your way slowly and steadily towards success. Strategic problem solving is your strong suit, and if you can consistently keep your positive attitude, you can become a powerful leader.

Weaknesses

When a Sagittarius-Capricorn cusp is not at their best, they become moody and closed off. They can be intense with their interactions, and when things go badly, they can become selfish and impatient. People can interpret that in a negative way and make you seem like an isolated individual. With all the hard work and passion that you put into your work, you might have no time for the people who are a part of your life. Although you are extremely helpful and loyal to the people in your circle, you might lack the emotional balance that a true friendship or companionship really needs.

Compatibility

Being a part of the Sagittarius-Capricorn cusp or the Cusp of Prophecy means that you have strong leadership qualities, often teaching others and being occupied with your talents and the things that interest you. To be able to develop a strong romantic relationship, you should seek someone who is a good listener and is willing to learn from you and understand you as a person. Fire signs will encourage your hard work and drive, encouraging you to become better and more capable. Earth signs will also help you keep a foot in the real world and appreciate your reliability.

Key Takeaways

Isolation can happen inadvertently, so try not to cut off the people in your life, even though that may seem very tempting in certain scenarios. Professionally, you are a capable worker who can come up with brilliant ideas that can help you become highly successful in the workplace. Small talk is not something that you will be very fond of, and you need fun and philosophical conversations to inspire you to live up to your potential. Focus on your friendships and personal relationships, and you will feel extremely satisfied with all aspects of your life.

Chapter Three: Capricorn Strengths and Weaknesses

In this section, we will delve into the Capricorn's key traits, both positive and "challenging." If you have a Capricorn in your inner circle, you may notice that they tend to do things that you definitely dislike or like. And if you are a Capricorn yourself, you may relate to the things mentioned here.

For instance, the Capricorn has no trouble approaching strangers at parties and is comfortable chatting away to the staff at a store. They'll say yes when you propose to go out and don't have that "I just want to stay home" default other signs have.

Now let us look at the positive as well as negative traits of the Capricorn personality.

Strengths of Capricorn

Hardworking

This is one of the most positive traits of a Capricorn personality. They are more diligent and serious than any other sign in the zodiac. People from this sign persistently work at any task they take up. If they are given homework at school, they make sure to get it done properly.

If they have a test coming up, they work hard so they can get the best score possible. If they are given a project at work, they spend a lot of time ensuring it is carried out efficiently.

That a Capricorn never gives up is one of the most admirable things about them. Even if they are not naturally talented at something, their persistence gives them the chance to do well at it. Their can-do attitude is enough for them to succeed in life. Capricorn individuals are always willing to learn something new if they think that it will bring them closer to their goals. This is why it is important not to underestimate the tenacity that Capricorns have.

Ambitious

People from this zodiac sign tend to have very lofty goals and are ambitious in life. They set goals they make sure they can achieve. They know that hard work and persistent effort will get them where they need to be. This sign is always driven to improve. They want to do better than they did yesterday, and they want to do better than those around them. This competitive ambitiousness keeps them going on the toughest days.

Even if they have to put in a lot of long and exhausting hours, they will do so to get what they want. They expect material rewards for their hard work, and this could be in the form of anything from money to fame. A Capricorn is one of the best partners to have with you on a school or work project.

Responsible

A Capricorn is also a very responsible person. They tend to be a lot more mature than other signs of the same age. They approach things in a disciplined and pragmatic way. Capricorns like staying organized and tend to follow the rules. They like taking the straight path even while working endlessly towards their goals. If a Capricorn makes a mistake, they are quick to learn from it and own up as well. They accept their mistakes and thus surpass these hurdles quicker than most. They are also very reliable for remembering important details like passwords.

Honest

Capricorn individuals don't see the need to lie. It is rare to see them be dishonest about anything. If they ever do lie, they will own up to it just as quickly. This positive trait in a Capricorn is one reason their relationships are stronger. They make it easy for their spouse or friends to trust them, and they make sure to keep their trust. This is not a sign that will cheat or lie to you.

Calm

It is great to have a Capricorn on your side during an argument. They always keep their cool and are good at handling pressure. Their calm and analytical nature makes it difficult for someone to win an argument with them. They can always counter fiercely with facts that no opponent can deny. They are good at protecting themselves as well as those around them by keeping a cool head in difficult situations. This is why they are also good at giving advice to others who are more emotional.

Weaknesses of Capricorn

Pessimistic

While being grounded and realistic is a good thing most of the time, it has to stop at a certain limit. If you are pessimistic, it will only make you focus on all the negative things in life instead of the positive. This is why pessimism is one weakness of a Capricorn. Their no-nonsense attitude often makes them miss out on good things. It leaves them feeling unhappy and dissatisfied in life.

Capricorns seem to get stuck in a negative cycle when they focus more on how things look instead of how they feel. Their constant need to succeed and come out on top leaves them very disappointed when they fail at something. Their need for perfectionism applies to everything in their life. They adopt a negative view of their future when they have to face any failures or feel like things are not perfect. This dejectedness and pessimism also have a negative effect on the surrounding people.

Workaholic

Being hardworking is a positive trait in Capricorn, but they take it too far and become workaholics. For a life to be well-lived, there has to be a balance between work and pleasure. Capricorns tend to push themselves to the point of complete exhaustion. They are too obsessed with perfectionism and success, and they miss out on a lot in between. They forget to take time off and relax as they single-mindedly pursue their dreams. Working hard is a great quality, but becoming a workaholic works far more against them than for them. They are too hard on themselves and compromise their mental and physical wellbeing.

Stubborn

Capricorn is a sign that is known to be extremely stubborn and set in their ways. While this sign thrives on diligence and ambition, it is hard for them to understand that not everyone feels the same way. This is why they often hold other people to their own impossibly high standards.

Capricorns are strict and value tradition to the point where it is difficult for them to accept any new changes. They struggle with opening their minds to new things. They find it difficult to look beyond themselves since they are always focused on what is practical and realistic. This sign's stubborn mindset makes it very difficult for people from other signs to get along with them.

Guarded

It takes time for a Capricorn to open up to someone. They are very guarded and self-preserving. They don't give in as easily to emotions as the other signs, and this can be difficult for their partner to deal with. Capricorns take time to trust others and talk freely with them. They only become expressive towards their partner once they are completely sure of the relationship. This can often backfire and push away someone who might have had good intentions. Being this guarded can even leave them with no one to talk to, which can lead to depression over the years.

While these are generalized traits of a Capricorn, there are always exceptions to the rule, but these points can help you understand most Capricorn individuals better. Capricorn's great thing is that they are always willing to work on improving their weaknesses if they feel like it will benefit them or make them better.

Chapter Four: The Capricorn Child

Every sun sign has a certain set of personality traits associated with it. This is not only limited to grown-ups but applies to children as well. Learning about your child's traits based on their sun sign can make parenting a lot easier for you. It would help you in understanding and predicting their behavior. It would also make it easier for you to deal with different situations. Your child would belong to the tenth zodiac if they were born between 21 December and 21 January.

Reading a little about your Capricorn baby will definitely be helpful in their younger years. Even if you don't have a child yourself, it will help you understand and deal with any Capricorn child in your life. It could be your niece, nephew, or even your friend's children.

Traits of Capricorn Children

Here are traits that most Capricorn children tend to possess:

Adaptable

While you might expect most children to have difficulty adapting to certain situations, it does not apply to a Capricorn child. They have an amazing ability to adapt to different situations, and this takes a lot of pressure off their parents. Taking them to new places, meeting new people, weaning them off liquids and onto solids are all simple processes. You won't have trouble with potty training or teaching them table manners either. Getting them to build good habits like doing their homework regularly will be a piece of cake. You might find that they don't accept things right at once because of their strong personality, but they take little time to adapt.

Persistent

Capricorn children are often mistaken as underdogs. People get surprised by what a Capricorn child can accomplish once he sets his mind to it. You might expect something to be out of their league, but if they want it, they will chase after their dream until they achieve it. They don't give up on things that genuinely interest them or are important to them. Another great quality is that they stick to their principles but don't preach to others about it. They don't compromise on things they consider important.

Ambitious

Capricorn children hold their dreams close to their hearts. Even if it seems to be an unachievable dream, you cannot shake them off it. They are ambitious, and their persistence helps them achieve their dreams most of the time, but they don't share their dreams or ambitions with many people. Only those they trust or are close to will know of it. These children will do a lot to achieve their goals.

Old Souls

A Capricorn child is not known to throw tantrums or act up. They are usually quiet and appear to be well behaved. You will see that they behave a lot more maturely than other kids of their age. This is why they are called old souls in a young body. Parents with Capricorn children will barely face any issues during the growing years. These children are calm and collected. They are also great at adapting to changes and are not easily shaken by unpredictable situations.

Perfectionists

Children of this zodiac like perfection. You will see they always finish their homework on time and that they keep their books and belongings in place. They like having their room clean and well kept. If you go about it smartly, you can take advantage of this perfectionist trait in your child, but if they learn of your intentions, they might want to rebel.

Predictable

As you spend more time with your child, you will notice patterns in their habits and behavior. It is easy to predict what a Capricorn child will do in most situations. If they trust you and can confide in you, they will share their thoughts with you, but if you can't build trust, it can be difficult to guess what is going on in their mind.

They Follow Rules

This is another reason it is easier to bring up a Capricorn child. They seem to have inborn respect for rules. Once you teach them what is right and wrong, they will follow these norms. They also have good intuition in judging what is right. Their deep regard for rules often makes them come across as conservative when they grow into adults, but they sometimes break the rules if the situation calls for it. If your child seems to break a rule, you should ask for an explanation. They usually have a very good reason for doing so. If you still feel like they were at fault, you can make them understand by using good reasoning and logic. This will help you get the point across to these little adults.

They Need Respect

Even as children, Capricorn children have a major need for respect. They dislike being treated disrespectfully. They also tend to think that they have to prove themselves so they can earn respect and love. This is why they try their best to follow the rules and work hard, but you need to tell your child that they deserve love and respect even if they don't always come out on top. Show them that you respect their goals and thoughts, but you also need to let these emotional beings know that they are loved despite everything.

Capricorn Kids at Home

As I've already mentioned, Capricorn children are wise beyond their years. This is why you need to treat them a little differently than other average children. They are serious, even at a very young age. You will notice that they ask deep questions that are more suited to adults. They are also quite sensitive to a deviation in their regular routine. It is better not to leave your Capricorn child with an adult with which they are unfamiliar. It is usually a little beyond their comfort zone. You can help them with this one step at a time. Another thing to notice is that Capricorn children usually dislike loud noises. It is advised to avoid subjecting them to such noises or leaving them with strangers too often as a toddler.

Once a Capricorn child gets interested in something, they can be a little obsessive about it. If they like to play with trains, they will probably want to read every book or watch every show related to trains. If they like dinosaurs, they will soon learn the names of every species. Don't be surprised if they often beg you to take them to the museum instead of wanting to go to the amusement park.

When you see your child take this much of an interest in something, encourage them. Express your interest and support for the things they love. This is one of the best ways to help them learn more as a child. Learning always begins at home.

When they grow into their teens, you might see that they are often critical of you or others at home, but this is only because they have a strong sense of what is right and social justice. They are not shy about expressing differences in opinions over such matters. As a parent, you have to learn not to take it personally. Instead, you can contact them by showing interest in their hobbies or by trying to initiate activities together.

For instance, if your teen likes to read, you can read the same book and have a discussion over it. If they like certain movies, you can show an interest and ask them for recommendations. These are easy ways to connect with Capricorn children. They are a lot less likely to want to talk about serious feelings or thoughts at this point in their life. So you need to work on building bridges.

While they act like little adults, they also have a silly streak. Try to draw it out much when they are children. Encourage them to play often and to do things they enjoy instead of focusing solely on schoolwork. While academics are important, they also need to learn other things. Instead of signing them up for competitive activities or events all the time, help them participate in collaborative ones.

They should learn to communicate and socialize with other children. Most Capricorn children prefer sticking their nose in a book instead of running around with other kids. If you don't help them participate in group activities, they may get lonesome. As a Capricorn parent, you have to give them room to grow and encourage all their interests. Express appreciation for the small things and not just for the big wins. This will help them grow into confident adults. Be expressive with your love and watch them grow into a caring and empathetic Capricorn.

Capricorn Kids at School

You will see that your child finds it easy to adapt when they start school. While it is normal for them to feel a little uncomfortable in the first few days, they soon get used to it. It will not be difficult for you or their teachers to help build good study habits in them. You will see they like keeping their books neatly and they mostly have good handwriting. You won't have to clean up after them since they like keeping their desk and room well maintained.

Capricorn children are ambitious and work hard for their goals. These go-getters can be competitive, so it will be difficult to console them when things don't work in their favor. They hate seeing an 'F' on their report cards, and they don't like coming in last in anything. You have to explain a lot and help them understand that it is okay to fail at times.

Mostly, they do well in school. If they show an interest in a particular subject, encourage them to pursue it. They may even take it up as a career once they grow older. Once they set a goal, it is nearly impossible to change their mind. They persistently pursue their interests as far as they can.

Capricorn children like having tasks to do and often get listless when they are free or bored for too long. Help them stay engaged with schoolwork, games, and other activities often. This will help them learn more and will also make it easier for you to keep them happy.

What a Capricorn Kid Needs to Thrive and be Comfortable

Capricorn children are not very troublesome to raise, but you should understand them and help them feel loved and comfortable. As a parent, it is your responsibility to learn how to help your child thrive in their environment.

Consistency is important for Capricorn children. While you have to teach them to adapt to changes, you also need to avoid exposing them to more than what they would be comfortable with. Try not to change their schools too often. It can be hard for them to leave behind friends and make new ones. This applies to changing homes as well. They like a routine they are familiar with. Continuity comforts them. Capricorn children are better at sticking to schedules than their parents usually.

Help your child grow up with a lot of nature around them. Capricorns have an inborn affinity towards nature. If you let your child out in the yard or in a park, they can easily spend hours amusing themselves. Nature is nurturing for them. It is also the place they like to retreat to and think.

These children are ambitious and practical but love being rewarded. When they do well, remember to reward their achievements. Also, remember to be kind and console them when they fail. Praise their little achievements the same as you do their big ones. Also teach them the value of things with little examples. Give them a piggy bank to store away any pocket money they receive. Teach them to spend only on things they need or want instead of splurging on useless things. They will pick up these habits as a child and do better as an adult this way.

You also should teach your child to be flexible. Capricorn children can be stubborn, and it would not benefit them to see things only in one way as they grow up. Help them understand the importance of looking at situations from different perspectives. Teach them how to act appropriately in various situations. Being one-tracked all the time may inhibit their growth.

Understanding a Capricorn child according to their gender:

Capricorn Girls

If you have a Capricorn daughter, it is easy to notice how they seem to act and talk like adults from a very young age. She never seems like a child. Even as a toddler, you will find her obstinate. These girl goats can charge head-on when challenged. You will also learn there are two sides to these children.

A Capricorn girl is usually carefree and happy, but it can be quite sad to see them in their melancholic moods. They lose all their fighting spirit when they are low. You have to give them a lot of extra attention and shower them with love in such moments. This melancholic side of your Capricorn daughter may be a little hard to deal with at times, but this is one of the rare hitches in her personality. These children are not high maintenance, and they are not very peevish. You won't have to deal with tantrums over dinner or the clothes you bought them. They will eat whatever they are served and wear anything you give them. They also love to organize, so get the toys that help her play in the way she likes.

As a Capricorn, your daughter needs to feel in control. You have to give her tasks to do so she can fulfill this need. She will appreciate having an established routine to follow. Give her a few simple chores, even as she grows. The love for continuity causes Capricorn children to get off balance when there is a disruption in their routine. But you have to help them overcome it so they can adapt well as adults.

You will also notice that your mature daughter prefers playing with older children a lot more than those her age. She likes having conversations with or hanging around adults. Her communication level is usually above other children her age if they are of a different sun sign. Once your daughter finds a friend she likes, she will hold her/him dearly for life.

While playing, you will see that your daughter prefers games with a purpose. Instead of playing tag, she would rather dig into your garden. Instead of playing in the sand, she would rather read a book. A game that helps her build or create something would be better suited for her.

While Capricorn children do well in school, you might see she misses deadlines at times. This is because a Capricorn child likes doing things in their own time and with their own approach. As a perfectionist, she might take a lot longer to complete her tasks. She will also be averse to any nagging or constant reminders to do things. You have to teach her to follow deadlines, but it will be easier to get things done if you just let her do it her own way.

With manners, Capricorn girls are very well behaved. They act respectfully and kindly towards others. They don't have a tendency to display arrogance, no matter how much they achieve. They are trustworthy and dependable. You might see that she takes time to warm up to new people, but she will open up completely once she does.

Capricorn Boys

If you have a Capricorn son, you must remember that they need security. They do not like being disrespected even at a young age. As parents, you have to show authority in a respectful yet firm way for them to receive it well. Since they are more mature than other children their age, you should have a conversation that makes them feel like you are treating them like adults. If you make the conversation simple, it will only be taken in a negative way.

Just like a Capricorn girl, your boy is also an old soul. He will spend a lot of time and thought in figuring out his personal goals instead of wasting time. While a Capricorn boy is ambitious and goal-oriented, he also pays equal attention to his family. You will see that he can reach his goals a lot faster than most of his peers because of his sure-footedness.

Even while facing new challenges he will stay calm and composed, but he hates being ridiculed or misinterpreted. This shakes the balance for a Capricorn boy. It can often affect him for weeks on end, so it is important for parents to help in regaining balance again. Showing appreciation and attention at such times is essential to helping them.

A Capricorn boy child is quite well mannered. He pays attention to etiquette and good behavior. He always tries to present himself neatly. But even while they dress well, you might sense a certain degree of uncertainty in them. You must praise them a little to restore their wavering confidence. Show your appreciation for his appearance whenever you see him put in that extra effort.

You will also notice that these boys like keeping their room or things neatly. Unlike most other children, they won't leave their socks or toys lying around. They like making their bed and keeping everything in its place. They have their own sense of order, so avoid fiddling with their things. Allow them to create their own comfort zone. Keeping these things in mind will help you raise a happy Capricorn boy in their younger years.

Activities Well-Suited For Capricorn Children

A Capricorn child is wise beyond his/her years, and this is why they enjoy hanging around adults. Your child will appreciate having conversations with you. They also like feeling helpful to their parents, so don't shy away from assigning simple chores even at a young age. While they may seem like homebodies, you must encourage them to play with children their age.

If you take them to the playground, you will often see that they hang back instead of rushing to play with the others. As a parent, you must help them come out of their shell. Encourage open-ended games as a group. Also, avoid too many competitive games. A Capricorn child is competitive by nature, and it will often end in tears or sulking if they don't win at such games. Instead, encourage games that allow everyone to mingle and enjoy without being pitted against each other.

Capricorn children are easily drawn to books, so do your best to encourage the habit of reading. Don't let them spend too many hours doing this since it can make them grow into loners. But allow them to appreciate the joys of reading at a young age. It will help them learn a lot over the years. When they are toddlers or quite young, choose books that will help them learn good morals. This will help in building a foundation for their values. You can then allow them to explore other books of their liking as they grow older.

Chapter Five: Capricorn in Love

Now we get to the part many readers look for, the Capricorn in love and relationships.

If you are looking for a long-term relationship, Capricorns are the wisest choice. They are committed, reliable, and faithful. Even if the relationship is difficult, they are determined to make it work. If you are Capricorn or are in a relationship with one, it can be helpful to learn more about a Capricorn in love. This makes it easier to work on the relationship and make it stronger with time.

The Conventional Lover

Prudent and Loyal

They tread slowly and are rarely willing to jump right into a relationship. They take their time to observe the situation and only get involved if they think it looks right. They like having control over everything all the time. If they feel like they can't trust someone, they will never enter a relationship with them. But once they do, they are loyal and trust their partner wholeheartedly.

Financially Savvy

This is great for someone looking for a financially stable partner. This sign knows how to handle their money well and are skilled with finances. This is why they are also attracted to others who are wise with money and work hard to earn it. A lot of Capricorns choose to work at banks, as accountants or as managers. They like being friends or lovers with others who are similarly smart when it comes to financial matters.

Giving and Protective

They do their best to protect the things that they hold close to their heart. This applies to their material possessions and to the people they love. Being in a relationship with a Capricorn is great since they want to do their best to keep stability and protect their partner even if it is at great personal cost. They are giving by nature and don't hesitate when it comes to their significant other, but their protective nature can get a little possessive, and not every partner can deal with it. Individuals who are carefree and treasure their freedom will find Capricorns too restrictive and feel smothered. But people who want a reliable partner will appreciate this possessiveness in their Capricorn partner.

Controlling

This sign is a natural leader, and it is not because they consciously want to be dominant or get attention. They just like having control so they can do things the right way. This controlling trait can be a drawback in a relationship with people who are more spontaneous, but if their partner is a perfectionist, Capricorns find it easier to navigate things.

Passionate About their Relationship

It takes them time to relax and feel free with their partner, but their love is made clear once they do. But you cannot confuse emotion with passion. This sign is never a naturally emotional one. They consciously avoid any dramatic emotions and refuse to let emotions rule over them. It can be frustrating for their partners, who usually have to coerce the Capricorn into sharing their feelings. But if Capricorn is paired with a similarly practical partner, the relationship can be very strong.

How to tell if a Capricorn is in Love?

Capricorns are rarely a flirty type of personality. In fact, they find flirts unattractive. Their approach to romance is a lot more traditional, and they have a more authoritative bearing. If you are interested in a Capricorn, you will usually have to make the first move. If the Capricorn is interested as well, they will let you know directly, but if they are not as direct, there are other ways to tell if they are interested in you.

- They will try to take every chance possible to get close to you.

- They are always generous with you.

- They make plans around you and will change their schedule for you.

- They try their best to impress you.

- They try making themselves indispensable to you.

Not every Capricorn is forthcoming about letting their interest show. They do it through their actions and wait patiently to see if the other person is interested as well.

Strengths of a Capricorn in a Relationship

Capricorns know what they want, and they also know how to get it. They go through their lives at their own controlled pace and move step by step. Capricorns listen to their head more than their heart, and this is not always a good thing in relationships. Even though a Capricorn's practicality is not very exciting, it helps them get things done. They are traditional and take the well-worn path. This sign is trustworthy and reliable. They are the ones you can go to for advice.

Capricorns get uncomfortable when they feel emotions running too deeply in their relationship. This is why they start distancing themselves a little to avoid attachment, but they are considerate and good lovers despite being on the tame side. They take their time making love just like they do everything else.

Challenges of a Capricorn in a Relationship

One challenge that most Capricorns face in a relationship is that they find it difficult to express affection to their partner. They think there is a time and place for everything, and this applies to love as well. They dislike any public displays of affection, but this could be something their partner needs.

Capricorns need to be flexible and consider what their partner needs to feel valued. This sign can only overcome all their inhibitions when they find the perfect partner. They need someone who will help them get better at handling emotions and opening up more.

Capricorns also tend to hold on to a grudge for a long time, and this is something that none of their partners will appreciate. They must learn to forgive and forget. Forgiveness is an important aspect of a good relationship. If the Capricorn remains stubborn about everything and refuses to relent in any argument, it's difficult to sustain a happy relationship.

Dating a Capricorn

Do you have a crush on a Capricorn or are you in a relationship with one? It is completely understandable why someone would be attracted to this sign. They have beauty with brains and are the most ambitious and hard-working sign in the zodiac roster, but Capricorns can be elusive when it comes to matters of love. You need to know this if you want to date a Capricorn.

Planet Saturn was named after the titan who tried remaining a ruler by eating his offspring, and this is why Saturn is linked to daddy issues quite often. But on a more serious note, the 29.5-year orbit of Saturn signifies true adulthood for a Capricorn in their late twenties. This is the point where Saturn comes to the same position it was during the time of a Capricorn's birth.

Saturn's return to its original position is when you become your true self and gain control of your life. It gives you all the tough love that comes hand in hand with adulthood. But the intensity of Saturn is not known for Capricorn. This is why people from this sign feel obligated to work very hard from a very young age. They think that they must be responsible at every point in life. This helps them develop a great work ethic, and you can see this displayed in many prominent personalities like Michelle Obama and Greta Thunberg.

The resilience of a Capricorn is often what defines them. The sign of the Sea-Goat that can navigate land and water can overcome any hurdle in their life. Capricorns live their life with the big picture in mind, and they never let anything, or anyone gets in their way. To date this sign, you have to remember this. Even if they have the same feelings as you do, their practicality will make them choose what is better for their goals.

Capricorns are naturally great at navigating work relationships, but this does not apply to their personal relationships. They choose partners who appear to be perfect instead of taking time to see if they are really the right fit. They also use their business strategies to navigate their relationships. Capricorns have a premeditated view about who would be the perfect partner for them, and this leaves them disappointed in the end.

Someone who looks good and earns well is not necessarily the right partner if you just choose them based on these credentials, but

Capricorn will learn this the hard way. Once they do find the right partner, Capricorns can access true emotional intimacy.

When a Capricorn is in a relationship, they are completely committed to it. Capricorns don't commit to someone unless they are serious about it. They change their schedule to accommodate their partner and expect the same from them. Capricorns tend to have a very tangible and physical connection with their partner. In a relationship, they need quality time together. Capricorns are very work-oriented, and they want someone they can rely on. They need a partner who can give them stability and reassurance.

If you date a Capricorn, you also have to remember that they have great memory power. If you say something once to a Capricorn, they will always remember it. Even if it was an offhand comment, it leaves a deep impression on them. This quality has drawbacks as well as positives. It means that they are great at remembering birthdays or anniversaries. But it also means that they will remember anything hurtful you say to them.

This earth sign has very high standards and is never willing to settle for less than what they consider the best. Capricorns are attracted to people who are ambitious and resilient like them. They are also attracted to those with skills that they themselves are lacking. So if you want to pursue a Capricorn, put your skills blatantly on display for them to notice. They love a challenge and appreciate the best in others. But no matter what you do, try never to let a Capricorn down.

Don't make a promise and break it. Don't under-deliver on what you say to them. Even if you intend to do something, set the bar higher and surprise them by doing more than you said you would.

Compatibility

Capricorn is not a very romantic sign and is better known for being loyal, honest, and serious. They tend to be very focused on business and don't pay a lot of attention to pleasure, but if they find the right partner, Capricorns can be very devoted and dedicated to the relationship.

When it comes to compatibility, you have to understand that people from this sign will always consider practicalities even if they fall in love with someone. Some say that their placements impact relationships with different signs in the wheel of the zodiac. While Capricorn compatibility is explained further in the next section, let's learn a little about the best and worst matches for this sign.

Best Matches for Capricorn

These signs are highly compatible for a Capricorn partner:

Taurus

Capricorn is well suited for Taurus since they are both down to earth and practical. These earth signs place equal importance on materialistic wellbeing and can thus understand each other. They are a well-balanced couple with similarities and differences. Their similarities make the relationship easy for them while their differences help balance each other.

Capricorn is hardworking and ambitious and often forgoes pleasure for work. Taurus is a lot better at enjoying life and can often get lazy. While a Taurus helps a Capricorn relax a little, Capricorn motivates Taurus to work harder. Taurus is also adept at bringing out the sensuality of a Capricorn when they are in a relationship.

Virgo

This is another excellent sign for Capricorn to pair up with. Virgo is also an earth sign like Capricorn. The sharing of the same element between these signs allows their relationship to be harmonious. Technically, the relationship between Virgo and Capricorn should be just as pleasant as that with Taurus, but this particular pair can have a little more tension between them since Virgo has more nervous energy. In a relationship with Taurus, the latter takes on a stabilizing role for Capricorn. But with Virgo, Capricorn is the stabilizing partner.

Despite this, Capricorn and Virgo can be supportive of each other and balance things out. While Capricorn sees the bigger picture and sets long-term goals, Virgo is better at dealing with short-term tasks and taking care of details. This pair has a great romantic relationship, but they will also succeed if they work in business together.

Scorpio

Capricorn and Scorpio are similar in certain ways. Both are quite serious and are good strategists, but neither like making small talk and both prioritize work over pleasure. They can seem very much alike for someone looking in from the outside. In a business partnership, this pair can be quite formidable.

One aspect of this match-up is that they both are completely comfortable with each other. This is not just because their relationship is great; it is, and their differences only balance them out. The deeply passionate Scorpio is paired well with the seemingly unfeeling and pragmatic Capricorn. Capricorn provides stability to the relationship, while Scorpio helps soften Capricorn down.

Cancer

Pisces has, technically, better compatibility with Capricorn than Cancer, but by nature, these opposite signs are great partners for each other. The value they place on family life is one reason this opposite pair works well together. The entire family should take part in getting chores done at home, and they should all interact adequately with people outside their little world. Capricorn and Cancer symbolize this polarity. These concepts are known as Agora and Hestia in Greek philosophy.

In most cultures, they are tied to specific gender roles. Even though it is changing a lot in recent times, gender roles are deeply rooted in traditional society. This is why the marriage between a Capricorn man and a Cancer woman is quite traditional by nature.

But for a Cancer man and Capricorn woman, there will be a natural reversal of roles. This particular pairing will succeed only if both are comfortable navigating through the social consequences.

Worst Matches for Capricorn

Now let's look at the least compatible signs:

Leo

A relationship with a Leo will be the most difficult one for a Capricorn. There will always be a sense of competitiveness in the relationship, as both want to be leaders and are extremely different from each other. Leo is a royal sign regardless of any social status or background. A person from this sign will always crave admiration and attention. Their primary motive as a leader is just to shine; they don't just want to be in charge of getting things done.

Capricorns like being a leader because they need things to be accomplished. They don't have the same flair as a Leo and may even find it unattractive. Leo, on the other hand, may find Capricorn boring and dull. It is rare to see a relationship between the two since they seldom get attracted to each other.

Aries

Similarly, there is the issue of a power struggle with a Capricorn and an Aries as well, but a Capricorn can still find an Aries attractive, unlike their general view of Leos. There is a square aspect between Aries and Capricorn that causes friction, but this square also leads to a lot of sexual tension between the two. When you hear a story about two people who hate each other at first but wind up together, it is usually one where this square is present.

Aries and Capricorn both want to be in charge of the relationship. Both signs like getting things done but have different ways of going about it. Aries don't think much before leaping into a project. They have a lot of energy at the beginning of the project but can rarely sustain it throughout. Capricorns like taking their time and always think first before doing something. Once they start a project, they will want to see it through. These are the kinds of differences that make their relationship volatile.

Libra

Capricorn is also in a square relationship with Libra, but it is a comparatively less volatile relationship. This is because Libra likes avoiding conflict as much as possible. Partners from these two signs will be attracted to each other but constantly be annoyed as well. A Libra does not compete with a Capricorn like they would a Leo or Aries, but they do not like giving up control, even though it may not seem like it at first.

People from this sign are good at getting what they want without displaying an outward need for control. Their social graces charm people from most other signs, but this does not work on a Capricorn. Their indirect approach will only annoy a Capricorn, and the directness of the latter is frustrating for a Libra to deal with.

In the next section, you will learn more about Capricorn's compatibility with other signs in the zodiac.

Chapter Six: Compatibility of Capricorn with other Zodiac Signs

Compatibility is another detail to keep in mind when dealing with different zodiac signs. This is especially important for love relationships. Understanding the compatibility of a Capricorn with other signs will help you in many ways. You can use this knowledge to avoid relationships with certain people whose personalities and thoughts will utterly clash with yours.

You can also use it to foresee the odds that your relationship with a certain person will positively influence your life. The dynamics between a Capricorn and every other zodiac sign is unique in its own way. As you read on, you can think about your relationship with someone of a certain zodiac sign and infer whether you see the truth in what is given here.

Capricorn and Aries

Sex and Intimacy Compatibility

When it comes to sexual compatibility, things are difficult for this combination of zodiac signs. The ruler of Aries is Mars, while that of Capricorn is Saturn. These planets are usually considered archetypal opposites and karmic enemies. The contact of Mars with Saturn can result in a lot of objective and physical obstacles for a healthy sexual relationship. Saturn will put a lot of pressure on Mars and draw away its energy.

The relationship between a Capricorn and Aries couple will lack sexual desire. It will lead to feelings of incompetence and may even cause impotence in one or both parties. A relationship between Aries and Capricorn is often triggered by an unconscious need to be sexually restricted or held back, but as with most things related to a Capricorn, the Aries individual could, in time, achieve some sort of balance. Despite the difficulties in their relationship, they might be able to find sexual satisfaction to a certain degree, but by the time this happens, the Capricorn partner may lose their need and energy to take part in such intimate relations.

This is why such relationships tend to come to an end. The combination of these signs is not easy or light in any way and is especially difficult in matters regarding intimacy. Separation is the best way for them to find balance again. A couple with this zodiac combination may be attracted to each other but should usually stay at a safe distance due to their differences.

In the best-case scenario, the Capricorn partner can control their passion and support the libido of the Arian. The Aries partner could learn a lot about their body and its needs from their Capricorn partner, but this balance is rarely achieved, and these two personalities inevitably clash in one way or another.

44

Trust

Aries and Capricorn individuals are both "all or nothing" types. Trusting each other will come easy to them. Even if they have a lot of difficulties and misunderstandings in other aspects of their relationship, neither will betray the other's trust. But they also tend to take this trust for granted. They can lose sight of the things that they should treasure in their relationship. This is why one partner should always remind the other about the qualities in their bond that should be appreciated.

Communication and Intellect

Capricorn exalts the ruler of Aries, Mars. This is why Capricorns and Aries should stick to conversations about work, career goals, physical activities, or achievements. Other than these topics, these two zodiacs have no common ground. A Capricorn partner will rarely allow their impulsive Aries partner to form their own opinions. They don't consider their opinions practical or useful. They usually consider the behavior of their Aries partner quite unacceptable even though they respect the energy spent.

Capricorn individuals are well-grounded and thus can measure situations rationally. This rationality causes them to hold on to their opinion about the tactlessness or idiocy of the Aries partner, but this can be extremely difficult for the Aries partner to deal with since they have a strong need to be respected and to have certain boundaries.

Aries, on the other hand, lack patience with their Capricorn partner. It seems like they only want people who will be useful in their life and are otherwise boring. They also seem to lack emotions and compassion. In one way or another, both the partners will always be wrong. They will be stuck in an endless battle of egos and be unable to understand what they really need from their partner; but it can be difficult for them to come out of this relationship, despite the chances of better relationships to be found elsewhere.

Understanding

Capricorn and Aries will always have difficulty in understanding each other. Initially, both partners will look at each other as a goal they set for themselves. They will think that their partner can change and grow if they put in the effort, but the problem with individuals of both these zodiacs is that they have no desire to change.

Despite their unrealistic expectations from the other, they hold on to the image of the person they think their partner could become. This is why there is an apparent lack of understanding between these individuals. They are only in love with the false image of their partner they have created. They waste their energy and efforts in pursuing the change they want to see. There is an emotional disability in the relationship between these Saturn and Mars zodiac signs, but the problem is not really about lack of emotions. Instead, the real issue is a lack of acceptance and understanding. They have their own opinion of what is right and perfect and are too narrow-minded to expand these conceptual horizons. This is why they can't accept their partner as they already are, but want to see changes.

Values

Capricorn and Aries both value clarity, honesty, and independence. This is why their values are never an issue that causes trouble in their relationship. When it comes to how they view people outside their relationship, they are mostly in sync. They may have trouble with their own relationship because they don't share certain values. Even though an Arian may value endurance and persistence in another, they don't necessarily want to develop these qualities in themselves. They also don't want to be controlled by someone with such characteristics.

Similarly, Capricorns may value their partner's focus and speed, but it is not necessarily something they want in themselves. These qualities would hinder their ability to pay attention to detail or cause psychological needs to be left unattended.

Shared Activities

Aries individuals tend to love waking up early and exercising, but Capricorns will never be able to understand this need to run at five o'clock in the morning. Capricorns, on the other hand, can spend their whole night doing something boring, but Aries can never understand the value of this thoroughness. Being studious is only of value to the Capricorn individual, while Aries love the results of physical exertion in their routine.

The latter is quite impulsive, while the former needs to weigh things before acting. Both have difficulty in understanding the other's values, but they can both find activities they could enjoy participating in together. Both individuals appreciate the value of routine and keeping their body fit. This means that they can figure out a time of day that would be suitable for both of them to work out, together. It would be motivating and uplifting for both partners to do such activities together in their day. Indulging in such shared activities can be very helpful in improving their relationship with each other. It would also allow them to understand each other better.

A relationship between Capricorn and Aries will never be easy. They will always compete with each other, and there is no telling who will come out on top. Separation is the only time they will find relief, but if they stay together out of stubbornness, they will spend their lives banging their heads against the wall. Their relationship can only be a success if both are willing to respect each other unconditionally and stop trying to change what they don't like. If they decide to pay attention to what is already good in their partner instead of highlighting their flaws, they can truly complement each other. Unfortunately, their rulers have a malefic nature that will prevent this accepting and positive relationship. If people with this zodiac combination ever get together, they should try their best to let their partner live the way they like and be accepting of their differences.

Capricorn and Taurus

Sex and Intimacy Compatibility

When it comes to sexual relations, Capricorn and Taurus can be quite frigid. This is why they would make the perfect couple. When they partner with other zodiacs, it is hard for them to open up. This is why they feel the need to experiment more. In such relationships, Capricorns display ingenuity in sex, but when a Capricorn partners with a Taurus, they are able to relax more. This couple can get to know each other better and thus can find comfort in their relationship.

Capricorn won't feel like they have to put in extra effort, and Taurus will stop fearing the chances of getting hurt. Identifying the source of the problem in this intimate relationship lies in the understanding of the moon. Taurus exalts the moon while Capricorn doesn't like it. If the Capricorn partner has trust issues or doesn't fall deeply in love with the Taurus, it can prevent an emotional connection between them. This problem will be further intensified by Taurus individuals having the need to be loved in an unconditional way. This can scare their Capricorn lover away.

The gap between individuals in this zodiac combination is caused by their different approaches to love and sexual instincts. Capricorn supports Mars and prefers physical strength with initiative. Taurus has trouble understanding Mars and does not like aggression or initiative. This can cause a lack of emotions for the Capricorn in their sex life and will lead to frustration for the Taurus. It can even cause impotence and lead to a lack of desire in their relationship. If they don't hold on to intimacy in their sexual relations, it can cause problems for this combination of zodiacs.

Trust

Capricorn individuals never indulge in lies or tolerate it from others. They find lies unnecessary but are not necessarily judgmental about it. When a Capricorn lies, it is usually just to see if the other person can catch their lie, but in relationships, Capricorns prefer complete honesty. They want things to be true and clean with their partner. This is something that their Taurus partner can sense, and it allows them to feel secure in the relationship.

While a Taurus can sometimes feel the need to lie to their partner to hide certain things, that is not the case when they partner with a Capricorn. Venus rules the zodiac of Taurus and is exalted in Pisces. This is why they understand that secrecy is important in relationships. But when they are with a Capricorn, they can stay true to their love and have a good relationship for a long time.

Communication and Intellect

Capricorn and Taurus are different by nature, but they are able to understand each other quite well. They also encourage their partner to grow in the way that they need to. While differences can cause trouble for some combinations, here it makes them the perfect couple. Taurus and Capricorn complement each other in a subtle yet pleasant way.

Taurus is blessed with a deep understanding of the moon, but this is something Capricorn lacks. Fearing emotions can cause neglect of emotional needs. Taurus makes it their mission to teach their Capricorn partner about the importance of being kind to oneself. Capricorn contributes to the relationship by teaching Taurus about responsibility and working towards goals without being distracted by emotions.

Understanding does not always come easy for this couple, but this can be overcome with compassion and empathy. If they put in a little effort, this couple can support each other better than any other combination of signs. They are both earth signs, and if they reconcile their differences, they can create magic together.

Emotions

Both these zodiacs tend to be careful in matters of love. This is why you cannot say with certainty if they can find emotional fulfillment together. If they begin a relationship, they must overcome this pattern. The Taurus may not feel like there is a good emotional connection in this relationship, but it will be the opposite for the Capricorn, who will appreciate their Taurus lover.

Once the Taurus can dig deep enough and reach the Capricorn's emotional core, they will experience immeasurable satisfaction. At this point, the two partners will never want to separate again. The Capricorn will feel like their heart has finally been touched, and they will try their best not to let go of their Taurus partner.

Values

Both signs value the material world and can go far together. Capricorns are good at leading the way to success and achieving financial security. Taurus is good at motivating and creating. Regardless of their goals, together they will find it easy to achieve them. The only hitch is their approach towards family and emotions. The different sides of personalities should be observed as complementary and not destructive. This will allow them to coexist peacefully together.

Shared Activities

Capricorns seem to never stop working, while a Taurus can seem lazy. Capricorn needs to rest more than any sign in the zodiac. Since they are highly ambitious, they tend to drain their own energy reserves, and Taurus helps restore this energy. They help their Capricorn partner eat and live well by taking a break from work. The striving nature of the Capricorn partner can also be motivating for the Taurus. It helps them overcome their tendency to be lazy and instead work at creating something. Together, this couple can achieve a lot. They just have to find a balance between work and rest.

The relationship between a Capricorn and Taurus can be very deep and almost unreachable for other signs in terms of creative power. They are complementary in a gentle way. While others might find them boring, they live exciting lives together outside the eyes of the outer world. The Taurus partner can motivate the Capricorn to persevere while the Capricorn can teach the Taurus ways to achieve what they want. They can work hard and raise a happy family together. This partnership can cause an unbreakable bond, especially if they can connect emotionally.

Capricorn and Gemini

Sex and Intimacy Compatibility

According to Capricorn, sex does not require many words. But a Gemini likes to explain every position and has knowledge of the Kamasutra. The latter also has a fondness for outdoor sex. When these two partners come together, it can sometimes be unbearable to watch. Their sexual philosophies differ completely from each other, and this makes it difficult to maneuver.

If you want a Capricorn to experiment with their sex life, you have to work at opening their mind and getting them relaxed. For the Capricorn, being with a Gemini is like caring for a child who will undoubtedly cause trouble. This is how it seems to the Capricorn even though it isn't always true. While Geminis don't think twice about indulging in sexual activities at any place or time, the traditional Capricorn feels a lot more responsible for their actions.

Capricorns and Gemini are rarely attracted to each other, but sexual relations are always possible. When it does occur, Gemini will always find the Capricorn too stiff and uncreative. The Capricorn will find the Gemini too unconventional. The relationship between these two zodiacs is funny because they both find each other boring. While most people find Geminis fun and interesting, their lack of deep emotions and focus is a turn- off for Capricorns. This is why sexual relations between the two are best avoided. If it does happen, they will have to set many boundaries and be creative to make it work.

Trust

Typically, it is not easy to trick a Capricorn. Gemini's are usually quite flirty and find it acceptable to partake in what they consider light adultery, but Capricorns, who never indulge in adultery, do not share this viewpoint. They need to be able to trust their partner completely and need clear boundaries for what is right and wrong. They will trust their Gemini partner because of the deep trust they award their partner anyway, but they will only trust their own interpretation of the truth.

Geminis do not put a lot of thought into their abilities, while Capricorns always go one step further. This is why it is easy for Capricorns to read a Gemini. They can easily tell when the Gemini is lying or discover what they have been up to. On the other hand, Gemini will find it extremely difficult to read a Capricorn or catch them at a lie because they trust them completely.

Communication and Intellect

A Gemini is great at communicating with others. They can resolve all kinds of issues by talking it out with people, but this ability of a Gemini holds little value for a Capricorn. They recognize that most of the things the Gemini talks about lack essence, but these partners can still hold conversations together since Geminis have their own serious side that resonates with a Capricorn's personality.

Even though Capricorn is the most difficult and strict type of sign to deal with, Gemini shares common things with them. The great thing about Geminis is they seem to be able to talk about everything under the sun. If a certain topic bores you, they will find something else to talk about. Capricorn individuals prefer talking about things that have a deeper meaning. They look for the hidden meaning in things and admire others who can discover this meaning. They are not as focused on details as a Virgo, but they may still spend their whole lives analyzing such things.

Capricorns like to figure out the logic behind the smallest things, and Gemini can give them a whole list of such things to analyze. As long as there is mutual respect, and the two individuals don't judge each other as someone boring or stupid, the relationship can help them understand the world better.

Gemini can benefit from the secure and steady nature of a Capricorn that will teach them to be better at organizing their thoughts and actions. A Capricorn will help a Gemini take their thoughts one step forward and get better at managing their time. Capricorns can benefit from the childish approach that a Gemini has towards life. The serious Capricorn can learn this quality from a Gemini to help them live a happier life.

Emotions

Both the signs are not very emotional since Saturn and Mercury rule them. The real problem is that these signs don't spark emotion in each other. When they come together, they seem to be immune to the other's charm, but if these signs partner with any other sign that is not too emotional, they will feel awakened. There is very little that connects a Capricorn with a Gemini. The main emotional connection between them lies in Gemini's dark thoughts and the emotional distance that a Capricorn has.

Values

Any information, regardless of its form or shape, is valuable to a Gemini. They appreciate a person's ability to be creative with their hands, to talk eloquently, and even how someone implements their various ideas. For a Capricorn, the things that hold value are punctuality, stability, and honesty. These signs' independence is attractive to both, but there is not much else that coincides in their world.

Shared Activities

The motives of a Gemini and Capricorn differ immensely. Capricorns appreciate useful things. This is why they only like participating in activities that are useful in some way. They don't enjoy a walk just for the sake of it. But if it means they will live healthier or if it will get them to a specific destination, they can walk for miles.

A Gemini can walk without a purpose. They don't need to know where they may end up. They are spontaneous and need not stick to a path. They might set out to buy groceries but end up at a movie. While Capricorn likes dedication and routine, Gemini loves to learn new things. This is where they both have a connection in problem-solving and constructive learning. Despite this, they usually walk in different directions in life.

Pairing a Capricorn with a Gemini would give you a strange fit. They both want the qualities that the other possesses, but they fail to recognize it in their partner when they are together. Gemini seeks a person who will keep them grounded and add depth to their lives. A Capricorn can do this, but the Gemini will only look at them as someone boring and unmovable. Capricorns seek someone who will help them relax a little and find joy in life.

Gemini can do this but come across as superficial and uncontrollable to the Capricorn. If they overcome their inhibitions and prejudice, this partnership could be valuable for both. Their differences can help them learn a lot from each other. It can allow them to achieve any goals they set for themselves. But this is only possible if they completely open up and learn to recognize the good in each other.

Capricorn and Cancer

Sex and Intimacy Compatibility

Capricorn and Cancer are a case of opposite signs that bring with them a strong attraction. Their passions are awakened when they come together, and they can be perfect lovers for each other. Cancer needs the patience that a Capricorn has, as it allows them to relax and feel sexy. Capricorns appreciate the fact that their Cancer doesn't take sexual relations lightly and acts true to their emotions.

Capricorn individuals may have had many partners throughout the years, but they only stay with someone who is emotional and family-oriented. The intimacy that a Capricorn lacks is exactly what Cancer brings to the table. The sign of Capricorn lacks home, love, and warmth. Cancer can be highly compassionate and heal Capricorn. This allows Cancer to thaw Capricorn's cold emotional state and thus improve their sexual and intimate relations.

Trust

Capricorns are trustworthy, but they are not very trusting. The way they think is influenced by the Pisces sign in their third house, and they tend to panic when it comes to intimate relations. When they are involved with someone, they know that the partner has a need for trust, and they show this to appease them, but they only truly trust their partner after a certain period of consistency or if other people corroborate their stories.

A Capricorn's relationship with Cancer works because Cancer rarely has any ugly secrets to hide. The exaltation of Jupiter in Cancer causes them to have high moral values. If Capricorns can show their devotion to Cancer, Cancer will trust them completely. But they are sensitive to the fact that Capricorn is not as trusting. Despite this, they choose to be understanding and pretend that they are not aware of this. The difficulty a Capricorn has with trust issues is endearing for Cancer instead of being repulsive.

Communication and Intellect

The strangest factor that Cancer and Capricorn have in common is genetics. This is obviously not to be taken literally. It just means that they have the same image of relationships that their ancestors had centuries ago. It is believed that our emotional bodies have information stored about the emotions our ancestors felt but couldn't act on or understand. Capricorn and Cancer connect at this point. When they meet, they feel as though they are long-lost friends or lovers and not just two people who just met. They have an instant affection for each other that is warm and familiar.

Even if their circumstances were completely different while growing up, they might feel as though they shared their childhood. This sense of familiarity helps these signs connect and talk about everything possible. There is an unexplainable closeness between a Capricorn and Cancer, but it is even more inexplicable how that emotional bond will come through in the beginning.

Capricorn is wary, and from the perspective of Cancer, this can be difficult to approach. Unless they can connect on a deep level, these partners will appear to have opposite goals in life. Cancer can be a lot more needy or clingy, while Capricorn is more independent and career-oriented. This is regardless of the gender of both signs. If they focus on this difference and see each other in a negative light, they cannot be happy together. But if they overcome it and reach out to each other, they will be complete.

Emotions

The love story between Cancer and Capricorn is an unfulfilled one left behind by their ancestors. This may lead to very strong emotions between the two and seem like a dream come true, but a karmic debt has to be paid before this couple can find happiness together. These two signs represent the axis of Jupiter's exaltation. Their expectations from the relationship and each other are closely linked to their emotional states.

Capricorn is considered one of the least emotional signs, while Cancer is considered a highly emotional one. One should focus on a career while the other should be focused on the family, but once these two signs lay eyes on each other, their emotions tend to run wild. Their primal differences can make it hard for them to come together, but this couple creates a stable and secure relationship with time. It is difficult to reach the emotional depth of a Capricorn, but a Cancer may take this as a challenge.

If a Cancer pairs with a Capricorn, it usually leads to marriage and a family together, but this earthly love only ends well if they accept each other as they are. Trying to change their partner will only cause trouble in the relationship. They can have a much better future together if they avoid this, and if not, they will only tire each other out.

Values

Both signs value practical sense and stability. They are opposite signs, but their values are quite similar. Cancer and Capricorn both seek stability in their life. They want a partner who will provide them with a sense of security. This will make these signs value each other. They will appreciate that they both never give up or quit even when things get tough.

Shared Activities

When it comes to Cancers, they have no preferences for what their partner indulges in. They will be happy to let the Capricorn spend their time as they please if it is not imposed on the Cancer as well. Capricorn is a lot more specific about how time should be spent and will plan activities in advance.

The advanced planning gives both partners the chance to change their minds and decide on something else if they suddenly realize it is not something they want to do. As long as this pair shows respect for each other's personalities, they won't have trouble agreeing on things. Cancer will rarely be up for sacrificing their sleep for work, and Capricorn won't tag along for shopping trips to buy decor. They have to find activities that both will enjoy. If they respect such boundaries, their time together can be satisfying.

The deep-rooted need in Capricorn and Cancer to mend their ancestors' broken relationship allows them to relive an ancient love story. These sun signs can quite handle any karmic debt that needs to be dealt with. Once they do this, they can choose each other as their partners for life. When this zodiac couple comes together, there is a high probability of them ending up together.

Capricorn and Leo

Sex and Intimacy Compatibility

Capricorn and Leo both have a deep awareness of self. This is the one thing these signs have in common. A Capricorn is much more likely to find a Leo attractive than it being the other way around. It is rare to see a Leo being attracted to a Capricorn. Even if they do develop sexual relations, this couple rarely envisions a future together. Capricorn individuals are practical and cool-headed for the most part. Leo, on the other hand, is passionate and warm.

Not that Leo is completely impractical or that Capricorn cannot be passionate. However, these signs will see no common ground. The story of the rulers of these two signs is that of fallen egos, and they represent an archetypal conflict in the zodiac. It could damage their self-esteem and cause them to doubt their attractiveness and beauty. This may be caused by the fact that Capricorn fears the freedom of sexual expression possessed by Leo, which leads to insecurity in them both. These signs can rarely meet the expectations of each other.

The sex life of this couple can become quite boring. However, they don't realize that they are similar. For them to have healthy sexual relations, they need to try new things and be warm towards each other. If they fall in a rut, they remain in it for a long time. This causes a lack of confidence and loss of libido in both partners. In the end, there is no sexual desire in either partner.

Trust

Neptune falls in the sign of Leo, and this is something Capricorn knows. This is why they can clearly see behind any act Leo puts up. The Leo partner questions their own personality and motives when they see the depth that their partner will go to. Any lie told in this relationship will come right back, and so it is futile to indulge in them. The light of Leo shines bright in the darkness of Capricorn. There is nothing this pair can hide from each other. If either tries to lie or be secretive, it leads to mistrust. However, this pair usually chooses to trust each other in every situation because they have no reason not to.

Communication and Intellect

Capricorn and Leo have their own priorities in life. They have very different personalities, and it is not easy for them to come together. They often waste a lot of time trying to prove themselves right in any situation or argument. They fail to understand that they have their own role and mission in life to fulfill.

Instead of trying to change the priorities of their partner, they should focus on their own. It is actually better for both of them to have their own separate goals in life. They just have to try to accept the differences they have and respect each other. If they do this, their relationship can be fulfilling and satisfying. Capricorn can help Leo add depth to their lives and be more intentional. Leo can help Capricorns have a more creative view and be more positive in life. If these signs can make use of each other's abilities, they can accomplish any plan.

Emotions

Capricorn and Leo can have a very emotionally challenging relationship. This is not because of a lack of love between the two. It is more because of the fact that they love each other. Leo has warm emotions that can be cooled and buried easily. If they can't express their love, it can get them depressed. Capricorns need more time for their emotions, but the fiery emotions of Leo can disrupt this. This can make the Capricorn feel that their Leo partner is not right for them, even if they find them attractive or smart.

The way that both these signs build up their emotions is a problem in the relationship. Having time and patience is crucial for making their relationship work. However, Leo does not possess these qualities, while they are the forte of Capricorn. Without patience, it is impossible to reach the heart of a Capricorn. They take time to warm up to someone and express their emotions. If either or both these signs have experienced difficult relationships in the past, it is even less likely that they will fall in love with each other.

Values

Both these signs appreciate plans, organization, and presentation. Capricorn is a lot more capable of making plans and setting goals than Leo. Leo values this in the Capricorn since they themselves tend to go with the flow in most situations. However, Capricorns look for a partner with a calm and sensitive emotional center but fail to find this in a Leo. This only happens in certain cases. Leo prefers people who are openhearted, direct, and free with their smiles. If they judge the Capricorn as not having these qualities, there is no future for them as a couple.

Shared Activities

The priorities that these partners have will determine the activities they want to participate in. When a Capricorn wants to feel energized and vigorous, they will partake in anything that Leo chooses. The Leo will be willing to take part in activities of the Capricorn's choice only when they want to settle down. Good timing is very important in this relationship. If it is lacking, both partners will stubbornly resist doing what the other wants.

If Leo and Capricorn meet at the right time, they can get along well. However, if they share different priorities in life, it can be a problem for their relationship. If Saturn can be reconciled with the Sun, it can bring a lot of benefits. However, this is easier said than done. Capricorn can provide more structure to Leo's life, while Leo can help inspire creativity in the Capricorn. Even if their relationship doesn't end well, this could help them achieve what they want in their lives. These signs are very different, but it is impossible to stop them from achieving it if they have a common goal.

Capricorn and Virgo

Sex and Intimacy Compatibility

If Capricorn and Virgo were not both strict and stiff about sex, they could have a great sexual connection. Their relationship always seems to fall short of a certain degree of pure emotion. However, not that they lack understanding or patience for each other; there is rarely any sexual activity between this couple because they have more reasons not to do it than to do it. However, if they reach some synchronicity, the beauty of their sexual intimacy shows the kind of depth both signs are capable of. This comes across in the form of deep emotions they express during intercourse.

Both these signs look for a partner who takes sex as a serious act, not something superficial, and who believes that it should be cherished. This is a common ground for Virgo and Capricorn. Both partners also tend to be a little shy, and this can create more attraction between them. However, this is only possible if they meet at a central point. If their partner is respectful and reliable, Virgo is always willing to try new things and bring excitement into their sex life. Capricorn is a great fit for them only if both partners open up a little more at the beginning of their relationship.

Trust

Capricorn is a trustworthy sign, and this is something that most other signs recognize. This earth sign is reliable, honest, and never deceitful towards others. Virgo tends to be a sign that can be trusted as well, but they may be unfaithful if they lack faith in their partner. If they feel like they can trust their partner, Virgo cannot control their emotions and be vengeful. However, Capricorns can bring out the best in their partner and help them stay in a faithful relationship. It may take some time for both signs to get used to each other and build trust. However, once they do this, neither will break their partner's trust and the sanctity of their relationship.

Communication and Intellect

Virgo and Capricorn's conversations can seem very boring to onlookers from the fire or air signs. Other zodiac signs can rarely bear the flow of conversation between two earth signs. However, for these two signs, it is a completely enjoyable experience. They both have deep thoughts that they can share and discuss with each other. Seeing a similar depth of mind in their partner is incredibly exciting for both Capricorn and Virgo. They like exchanging informative and interesting facts and enjoy a respectful debate between themselves. They find the perfect adversary in their partner. These signs can complete a conversation in a satisfying way.

Capricorn is good at deciding when a debate is resolved while Virgo tends to decide on the next topic of conversation. They have a perfect system going for them. It is like gears fitting well and working without a hitch. Their intellectual conversations are where their passions lie. They find it very stimulating, and it keeps them happy together. Their communication skills are great, and they know that they can always talk it out. If there is a problem, they know that they can resolve it.

Emotions

Virgo and Capricorn are usually not emotional individuals. Capricorn is the zodiac of the moon's detriment, while Virgo brings the fall of Venus. Both these signs have their own emotional issues. However, their issues differ from each other, and this allows them to understand and help their partner. Just like the trust between them, it will take time for their emotions to build towards each other.

Time is of the essence in this relationship. Both partners will become a lot more confident as the passion between them slowly and steadily rises. Once they are confident, they feel a lot more liberated with their partner. They are open to experimenting with their sex life as well as in other things. This adds quality to their relationship. This couple takes time to slowly understand and discover new things about each other. As they peel away the layers from their partner, they notice things they missed before. It becomes a fascinating process for them and is an incredible aspect of their relationship.

Values

Capricorns and Virgos appreciate calm, cool, and collected behavior. No matter how complicated or difficult a situation is, they prefer to deal with it in a rational way. Since both of these signs are able to do this, they bring peace to each other. They also value the depth that their partner has and are grateful that they need not pretend to be shallow as with others.

Both these signs are well-grounded and practical. They like rational and sound decisions with regard to finances. However, the difference between them is that Capricorn will go to extreme lengths to achieve their goals while a Virgo will not. Seeing the extent to which a Capricorn goes can be too much for the Virgo at times. Capricorn will also find it difficult to understand the lack of motivation and competitiveness in a Virgo.

Shared Activities

Virgo is more focused on moving forward in life while Capricorn is focused on moving up. This is where these two earth signs differ from each other. They will have the same energy in following where their partner goes, but they rarely agree on the destination. This applies to activities they do together as well. It is important for these signs to find activities that will help them feel positive. They need a routine to keep them happy in life. If not, Virgo can sometimes make too many sacrifices and eventually become depressed. Capricorn is not always willing to take responsibility for what their partner does and is less likely to fall into depression with their partner.

Since both Capricorn and Virgo belong to the earth element, they can walk at the same pace. While other signs may feel like this couple moves too slowly, it goes exactly as needed for Virgo and Capricorn. They take their own sweet time to build their relationship with love, trust, and respect for each other. If they give each other some time, they can find the perfect partner in each other. They are also great at listening to what their partner needs and being willing to meet their expectations. Since they are both not emotional, their relationship may become a little too strict. However, this hurdle can be overcome with time as they grow out of it, spending their lives together.

Capricorn and Libra

Sex and Intimacy Compatibility

Waiting is the first thing that relates to the sexual relationship between a Capricorn and Libra. It is similar to a wife waiting for her ship-bound husband to come back after years at sea. Both Libra and Capricorn think of sex as an important aspect of their lives. However, these signs ruled by Saturn and Venus may have very little sexual activity as a couple.

At first, there may be a complete lack of attraction between them. Once they form a relationship, they discover the lack of sexual chemistry in their relationship. Even if the lack of attraction is not a concern for these signs, there will always be something that comes between them. This pair will have to deal with many factors out of their control. They will usually feel too pressured in the relationship, which could negatively affect their self-esteem. However, Saturn's exaltation in the sign of Libra could build an understanding between the two. It helps the couple understand the importance of good timing. It will also prevent them from making mistakes by having unrealistic expectations.

If Libra and Capricorn can overcome all other obstacles to form a bond, their sexual relations can be routinely approached and conservative. It will only bring satisfaction if both signs let go of any rules and strict premises.

Trust

This unlikely couple has a strangely high amount of trust in each other. While Libra may have questionable motives at times, their Capricorn partner will make them feel guilty about the slightest hint of a lie. However, if the Capricorn partner is too strict with them at the beginning of the relationship, it makes them feel judged and inadequate. This could lead to dishonesty in the relationship, even if there is nothing there to hide. The Libra is just secretive because they want to protect their privacy and themselves.

Communication and Intellect

Libra is not normally a very stubborn sign. However, when paired with a Capricorn, they suddenly become impossible to talk to and very headstrong. Due to Saturn's exaltation, Libra will love Capricorn a lot. However, they express this love unusually and seem to speak out of spite most of the time. This can lead to a never-ending battle between the two, with no one coming out on top. These two signs just keep building up walls even though they don't know why they feel the need to do so. The elements that these signs belong to can cause an obstacle to their understanding of each other.

Earth and air are far apart, and these partners can't reach out to each other. No matter the issue, they fail to understand each other. However, both signs have certain prudence that might allow them to have some interesting conversations and motivate each other.

As long as they remain rational, they can enjoy things with each other that most other signs would not find joy in. Both Libra and Capricorn would find immense satisfaction in solving a serious problem. Doing this together is possible if Libra uses their words and

Capricorn acts on them. Their egos would be at an all-time high if they can put in some effort to find a solution together.

Emotions

The way that a Capricorn and Libra approach their feelings is a difficult point for them to reconcile. Emotions come naturally to a Libra since Venus rules them. However, they are also serious by nature and tend to hold back their emotions because they fear judgment from others. Capricorn will be the judgmental force that can hold Libra down. This also feeds the ego of the Capricorn and makes them feel like they are always right. This takes them even further away from the point at which they can meet their partner.

For a Libra and Capricorn to make it work, they have to show that they love and respect each other. Since Capricorn is not very emotional by nature, it is difficult for most signs to reach out to them. However, for a Libra, this task is more difficult than it is for others. Libra will back off as soon as Capricorn dismisses their emotions. Finding a central point where they both show absolute acceptance and respect for each other is essential for this relationship to work. They have to let each other cry, get angry, break things, or even make scenes in public if it can help them be more expressive.

Values

Taking responsibility and valuing time is important for both Libra and Capricorn. These shared values help them overcome their opposing personalities and any differences. They know that they have certain responsibilities towards each other and will see it through. Being earth and air signs, they are set in their ways. They are very different in how they speak and what they do. Libra considers their mind of great value, and Capricorn doesn't care about words if they don't see results. Being with a Capricorn can help Libra put their words into action. However, the romantic relationship between the two will not be pleasant for either.

Shared Activities

Being boring to everyone else is the best thing that these signs can do together. It is likely that their relationship will make them work hard without being creative, and when they rest, they are lazy. It is important for them to create a routine that will help them go out together and do fun things. If not, their passion for each other will die.

The best way to describe a possible relationship between Capricorn and Libra is to say it is difficult. They may enjoy all the troubles that come with their coupling and even stay together for a long time. However, this is the kind of bond that most other signs will want to avoid. The real challenge in this relationship is that they don't respect emotional value. Both partners must figure out a shared language to express their love and understand each other.

Capricorn and Scorpio

Sex and Intimacy Compatibility

A special bond exists between Capricorn and Scorpio when it comes to sexual relations. Mars is a ruler of Scorpio, and Capricorn exalts it, thus causing the signs to be sextile. Capricorn's physical nature grounds the sexual needs of a Scorpio. However, these signs are the fall and detriment of the moon. This can cause a problem for the couple. Agreeing not to be too emotional or sensitive takes away any real intimacy from the sex life between these signs. They might enjoy their physical relationship, but they become cold and distant towards each other.

Even if they think that the physical relationship is enough for them, it won't appease their hearts. They realize their need for intimacy only when other people show up and fulfill this need. These signs are attracted to people from their opposing signs, Cancer, and Taurus. Those two signs are highly emotional in contrast to this couple. This attraction explains the need that Capricorn and Scorpio have for genuine intimacy that goes beyond the physical. They will not be truly satisfied until physical pleasure comes with emotions and tenderness.

The conservativeness of Capricorn can be frustrating for Scorpio since it exalts Uranus. However, they can take some time to help the Capricorn overcome their inhibitions and relax enough to try new things with their Scorpio partner. This sexual excitement will be difficult for the Capricorn to let go of. In return, Scorpio will appreciate the patience of a Capricorn and the sense of security they provide.

Trust

The one sign in the zodiac that Scorpio can completely trust is Capricorn. Being honest and direct, Capricorn will make Scorpio feel no need to be dishonest. The lack of true intimacy is the only thing that could cause distrust in this partnership. If they don't have depth in connection, they can't be sure about trusting each other. However, if both signs work on overcoming their insecurities and put some emotional effort into the relationship, this problem can be resolved.

Communication and Intellect

Capricorn is earthly, stubborn, and set in their ways, while Scorpio is constantly changing and evolving. This can be difficult for the Capricorn to deal with. They can understand each other well since Capricorn is patient, and they have a similar pace at which they do things. However, a disagreement between the two could cause a fight that lasts years.

The conversations between these signs are never easy or light. They both acknowledge the depth of mind in their partners and have a similar view on karma. However, you will rarely see them dance, laugh, or enjoy together. While the pair may think they don't need these things, it is not true. Everyone needs some fun and laughs in their lives. It is easier for the couple if they have mutual friends or share some dark humor. Capricorn can help Scorpio develop long-lasting friendships if they respect their crowd. Having the same group of good friends can be great for this couple.

Emotions

The emotional contact between Capricorn and Scorpio poses the biggest issue in their relationship. Both signs have their own emotional issues but dismiss them. At the beginning of the relationship, both will show their partners they are grounded and strong. However, they will fail to notice this impression will make them feel like they always have to be the strong one in the relationship. They will try their best not to show any signs of weakness even if they could do with some support. Both signs will drift away from achieving their emotional balance goal if they don't work on developing a deeper emotional understanding of each other.

Values

The values shared by this couple are interesting to observe. Capricorn brings guilt into Scorpio, the sign of the detriment of Venus. This means that their values are based on guilt, and they always feel like nothing is good enough. Although this can help them stay motivated and work on themselves, it can be difficult to deal with in the long run. They both need a healthy relationship that helps them accept that they are more than good enough.

Shared Activities

Capricorn and Scorpio strive for greatness together. Their energy will be focused on constructive activities so they can achieve the goals they have set for themselves. This relationship will not be an easygoing and joyful place where it is all rainbows and cakes. However, it is a great partnership to promote personal growth, realism, and practicality. If they share their past with each other, they can help their partner heal. They both like digging into the truth of things, and this will help them stay together.

Capricorn and Scorpio can share an inspiring relationship. They like to dig up family trees, search for the truth, and deal with any debt or unresolved karma. Both signs are deep and never take things lightly. They appreciate this in each other, and it helps to build a strong foundation for them. However, this depth and these values can also make their relationship lack emotion and become a little too dark. It could lead to depression or sadness and may even make them look for the light in someone else.

Capricorn and Sagittarius

Sex and Intimacy Compatibility

The sexual contact between this pair is somehow unbearable. Even if Capricorn and Sagittarius are attracted to each other and have sex, they will soon feel like they don't belong together. This feeling has no logical explanation but exists nonetheless between this pair. They can handle the differences in their personality quite easily since Sagittarians are easy going while Capricorns tend to understand their partner's immaturity as their own fault.

Capricorn seeks depth and meaning in their physical relations since they are patient and realistic. However, this pace is not something Sagittarians can always understand. They don't understand the importance of being as realistic as Capricorn. This pair won't be able to see their incompatibility at the beginning of their relationship. However, with time, it becomes obvious. Their differences will taint their sexual relations and make them realize that they are not suited to each other. Capricorn and Sagittarius can only have a healthy sex life if Capricorn loosens up, and Sagittarius starts respecting the physical. The meeting point for these signs is pure emotion.

Trust

Sagittarius is an honest sign when it comes to relationships. However, they have a problem for being honest with themselves. Capricorns notice this flaw and recognize that it is something that does not change in a Sagittarius. The problem is that Jupiter rules Sagittarius, while Capricorn is the sign of Jupiter's fall. Capricorn cannot comprehend the magic of life or any beliefs of a certain kind. They only trust in rational thought, hard work, and real results. However, Sagittarians believe that their positive beliefs can help them gain a good outcome in life.

Communication and Intellect

A Sagittarius and Capricorn should avoid talking or arguing about their belief systems. If they can do this, these signs are mostly quite understanding of each other. The optimistic smile of a Sagittarius can always bring a smile to the serious face of a Capricorn. Capricorn's practical approach helps the creative and fiery Sagittarius feel grounded. As long as this couple is respectful towards each other, they can build a lot together. Their vision is similar to builders, and they can bring their vision to life successfully.

Intellectually, they are a compatible pair as long as they don't expect any major changes from one another. These signs have complimentary protective roles, and this is the most beautiful aspect of their relationship. Both Sagittarius and Capricorn represent protection. If this couple builds a functional core together, they will never allow any outsider to impact their relationship. This pairing is the best choice for both signs if they are searching for partners who won't allow other people to meddle, interfere, or disrespect their relationship.

Emotions

It is possible for these signs to share an emotional language. This is because Capricorn looks for someone who will complete them, and Sagittarius becomes that person since it is where Jupiter is exalted. The heart of a Sagittarius and Capricorn come together at this meeting point. They can fall deeply in love with each other with some faith and avoidance of unrealistic expectations. Capricorn usually needs a tender and mellow person as a partner, but Sagittarius is rarely of this temperament. However, by understanding differences and becoming close, this obstacle is easy for the pair to overcome.

Values

Another common ground for Capricorn and Sagittarius is that they value intelligence. Sagittarians focus on learning and philosophy as they seek unity and the universal truth. Capricorn is a sign that is able to use knowledge in a practical way. This makes them a good pair. They can have the same wavelength if they don't think of each other as stupid.

Accepting each other will allow them to see that they have a similar depth of thought and share certain values. This is not possible if they judge each other at first glance. However, most of their values are still quite different, and both signs have very different needs as well. One places more value on responsibility, practicality, and focus while the other values creativity, freedom, and width of scope.

Shared Activities

You might think that a Capricorn partner would be too boring for a Sagittarius, and this might cause the latter to run off. However, this is not what happens in most cases. Since their suns share no relationship, these signs are respectful towards each other. This is why Sagittarius finds Capricorn interesting despite their differences. Their differences make these signs curious about each other, and Sagittarius, in particular, is always up for trying new things.

Sagittarius partners tend to enjoy a lot of childish activities that a Capricorn will refuse to participate in. However, they like to talk their serious Capricorn partners into these things in a joyful and fun manner. Both signs are smart and are aware of the differences between them. This makes their partnership a lot more refreshing and exciting for them.

The coupling of a Sagittarius and Capricorn is not ideal, and they rarely choose each other as their life partners. However, their relationship can be enjoyable and refreshing since both accept and understand each other despite their differences. No matter how short the duration of their relationship, they will have a good time together. This relationship will only be stable if the Capricorn puts in the effort to help the cause. However, the Sagittarius partner will always be able to bring joy to the Capricorn and acts as the pillar in this pairing.

Capricorn and Capricorn

Sex and Intimacy Compatibility

It can be difficult to predict the sex life of this couple. Being of the same sign, they will both exalt Mars. This means that they have strong libidos and like following their instincts. However, Capricorn is a sign that tends to hold on to restrictions. This pair may prefer making rational decisions instead of giving in to their instincts and looking for satisfaction. It is difficult to pair sexuality with practicality.

Capricorn is a lot more sexually creative when they are in a relationship with other signs, and they are also able to form a more intimate bond. However, when a Capricorn is in a relationship with someone from the same sign, they rarely satisfy their sexual or emotional needs.

Capricorn is also a ruler of time, and this means that this couple can end up waiting for a long time for things to happen. Since they exalt Mars, they won't lack initiative. However, in matters of sex and taboos, these partners can't seem to actually get to the point of sexual contact. If two people from this sign come together, their relationship may be extreme in two different ways. They might need very few words to understand each other, or they may never be able to understand what their partner means or needs. There is no middle ground for them.

Trust

As a Capricorn, it is easy to trust someone from the same sun sign. However, there is also a need to compete even in this matter. Both partners will feel like they are better and more honest than the other. This can make it difficult for them to build trust in the relationship. Lies are never a real issue in the relationship between two Capricorns. The problem is the silence they leave between them. When they try to communicate, both partners tend to leave a tense atmosphere between them, and this makes them question each other. The silence makes it difficult for them to identify with their partner.

Communication and Intellect

Capricorn is an intellectual sign with a lot of depth. This means that two people from this sign will have a lot to talk about. However, these conversations will rarely last long. Being extremely competitive, they will always end up in a debate. Instead of a prolonged debate, it turns into a silent tournament that neither wins. This couple needs to be open and speak their mind with each other. If they choose to silently analyze each other, they will not get far but instead, lose respect for their partner.

Most of the time, Capricorn partners will not feel the need to talk. Both will be interested in their partner's lives and would have many things to say. However, they don't share much since they seem to constantly have a fence up. When they work on a project together, it gives them the chance to talk, and this is when they discover how much they have in common.

Working together is the best way for this couple to have meaningful conversations and communicate. Having similar minds, they will be a lot more efficient at solving issues together. They can enjoy their conversations if they continue doing this.

Emotions

The emotional contact between two people from this sign is quite interesting. Both lack the ability to be emotional most of the time, and they will always try to be rational, cold, or controlling. They will recognize the same traits in each other, and this will only annoy them further. However, the great thing about this partnership is that they share the same values and approach to relationships. They will take their time to get to know each other and open up. Once the pressure falls away, they will feel safe in the relationship and be better at expressing themselves.

If this pair falls in love, it will take time to say it out loud. This is because Capricorns tend to dread any emotional displays. They are not confident enough to do this in private or in public. If they show each other some understanding and boost each other confidence, it will be a lot easier to be emotionally expressive. However, this will not be easily achieved, even if they respect each other. This couple will be more comfortable in silence and by letting each other be. They can understand each other because they are similar, but it will cause a rift between them if they don't work on their emotional connection.

Values

You may think that members of Capricorn share all the same values, but it isn't so. Every Capricorn individual can have their own values, and these are set in stone for them. It can be difficult for two Capricorns to share these values. If certain behavior doesn't appeal to them or they consider it wrong, they won't accept it even in the case of their partner. All their rules and values apply to any individual they come across. This couple should avoid questioning their partner's different values and instead focus on the values that they do share. Judging each other on such differences will only cause a rift.

Shared Activities

Although both Capricorn partners can easily participate in an activity together, one or both will refuse to. Even if they have the time to do it, they seem to avoid participating in shared activities out of spite. There is no other logical explanation for it. You would think differently since this sign is usually quite responsible and loyal. However, at the beginning of the relationship and until they loosen up towards each other, it will be difficult to get them to do things together. Once they do, they can actually see that they like doing a lot of similar things and will enjoy doing it together.

However, Capricorns are not great at understanding what their partner from the same sign might need or want. They have to be close enough to achieve this, and if they drift apart, they lose any understanding of each other. When this happens, the couple might choose to separate and instead look for partners from different signs who are more mellow and compassionate.

It isn't ideal for a Capricorn to be with a partner from the same sign. Two negatives sometimes give a positive, but with Capricorns, it is far more likely to give another negative. When one dominant Capricorn comes together with another, the relationship is not very functional. Both want to come across as the superior one, which will eventually lead to their relationship ending.

If they really want to make it work, they have to focus their sense of superiority and competitiveness outside their relationship. This will help them maintain balance in the relationship. If they don't stop locking horns, they might end up with different partners.

Capricorn and Aquarius

Sex and Intimacy Compatibility

Aquarius is the opposite of Capricorn, which is restricting and traditional. However, the same planet rules over both signs, and this means they also have similarities. The problem in these partners' sex lives is that they have a different pace because of their different elements. Capricorn is a thorough and slow Earth sign. This partner will only jump into a relationship with someone they respect and are attracted to.

When they have sexual relations, Capricorn will try to give it their best. Aquarius is an unreliable and slightly flaky Air sign. This is despite the fact that the master of reliability rules them. Aquarians don't think too much before jumping into a relationship and are quite spontaneous. They like things to be relaxed and not too serious in the beginning. This sign is rarely patient enough to go at the same pace as Capricorn. Capricorns like taking their time and making a plan, so the spontaneity and casualness of Aquarius can be a turn-off for them.

Capricorns don't like having sex hastily, so they don't rush into it with someone. Both signs are very passionate with the right partner, but the beginning plays a big role in how the relationship will work out. It is difficult for these two to reconcile since their approach is so different. However, they can become good friends since they have respect for each other. They can even have a sexual relationship as friends if they communicate well with each other.

Trust

Lies are not a big issue between these signs. Capricorns are set in their convictions and hate being wrong or making mistakes. Aquarius does not fear confrontation and places value on truth. This is why neither sees any reason to lie to each other. However, they both have different ideas of trust. It can be hard for them to accept each other.

They may believe that both are honest but not believe that their relationship will work out. They only lack trust in their relationship.

Communication and Intellect

If you belong to a sign like Cancer or Taurus, it can be difficult to bear the intellectual relationship between Aquarius and Capricorn. Both silently but distantly respect each other. However, they keep growing further apart as they try to maintain this respectful relationship. They don't want to see each other in a different way and would rather separate than change the way things are.

This means they are far more likely to be lasting good friends. But it is important to remember that these signs are very different. They find it difficult to understand the way their partner lives. Their relationship can only last if they have a mutual love for a serious bond and shared interests.

Emotions

Capricorn and Aquarius have a strange emotional side. Both signs are usually quite unemotional and stay detached from others they are not close to. But this closed nature is not the reason that their relationship lacks emotional connection. For Capricorn, emotions need to be expressed in a practical and physical way. This earth sign is often called selfish since they place their own needs first.

Spiritual signs tend to find it difficult to accept the earthly nature of Capricorn. They don't understand the need for anything material or even money. Being an air sign, Aquarius has ultimate faith in everything. Their faith is not focused on any rules or religions that man has created. They want a partner they can share their floaty ideas and heavenly love with. They don't have an attachment to food, money, and even sex. They want to dream and live carefreely. For Aquarius and Capricorn to bond emotionally, they have to accept the difference in their partner's reality.

Values

Aquarius needs freedom, while Capricorn places value on boundaries. This is why it may seem difficult for them to be in a loving relationship. But Capricorn precedes Aquarius, and there has to be some pressure for them to feel liberated. These partners come together in a strange way, but they realize they value the same things if they get closer. Both want loyalty and consistency from their partners. They also tend to have the same requirements while looking for a partner. Both signs dislike being with someone who tries to control them. Their needs from a long-term partner are surprisingly similar.

Shared Activities

Neither sign lacks energy. Capricorn is good at knowing where they should spend their energy. Aquarius is unsure of what to do with all their energy. This couple may not want to do the same things often, but they can take time to find activities they will enjoy together. The Aquarius partner should avoid insisting or trying to force their Capricorn partner. The latter should avoid trying to deny, restrict, or inhibit their Aquarius partner.

Aquarius and Capricorn may not be instantly attracted to each other at first. Though Saturn rules them both, they have different roles in the zodiac. The emotional contact between the two signs is the most challenging aspect they have to deal with. To stay together, Capricorn needs to be a little less grounded while Aquarius has to be a little less flighty. Finding a middle ground can be beneficial for both. Aquarius can learn how to act on their ideas from a Capricorn while Capricorn will be able to learn something new and bring some changes into their life.

Capricorn and Pisces

Sex and Intimacy Compatibility

If a Capricorn really wants to be relaxed in their relationship, they need to find a partner from the Pisces sign. The sexual relations between these two can be great since both are powerful in their own way. Capricorn is rational and strict, while Pisces is emotional and flexible.

Despite being different, they both are confident about what they believe in. There is a strong attraction between these two signs. If you observe the characters of these two signs superficially, it can be difficult to explain their sex life. However, Pisces can emotionally connect to a Capricorn in a different way than Cancer. It is more about their deep inner truth rather than passion.

Even though Capricorn seems to be a cold sign, they do not completely lack emotions. Although it may seem that Pisces is lost in their emotions, they can be quite rational at times. These signs can bring out the best in each other. Their rational-emotional understanding allows them to share a deeply intimate bond.

The sexual relationship between these two signs can be very spontaneous. Pisces will inspire Capricorn to open up and let go of their inhibitions. Capricorn will help pieces act more grounded and show their affections in a physical way. Pisces will get more serious while Capricorn will loosen up a little during the course of this relationship. If they can stay together for a long time, their relationship will have trust, stability, and emotional excitement in the perfect amounts.

Trust

Capricorn and Pisces will usually steer clear of any dishonesty if they understand and respect each other. However, there is still a chance for them to hit some rough patches. The rough nature of

Capricorn can make the Pisces partner feel the need to lie at times. But if the Capricorn acts unreachable and closed up, they will fail to understand each other. The approach to trust that these two signs have is what makes their relationship beautiful. Both are wary of opening up to the world, and their trust has to be earned day by day. This is how both slowly come to trust each other and connect over time.

Communication and Intellect

Pisces partners can be very inspiring for Capricorn. Both care about good communication in a relationship. They like to be the ones talking, but they learn to stop and listen in this relationship. Since both are shy to a certain level, they have to pay attention to each other if they want to learn more about their partner. Both will do this and are genuinely interested in getting to know their partner in depth. However, they face a problem when Capricorn acts rigidly over their beliefs or opinions.

While Jupiter rules Pisces, Capricorn brings this planet to its fall. They can endanger the relationship between these signs. The simple disbelief of the rational and strict Capricorn can greatly damage Pisces' faith in their own convictions. Pisces live for their belief system and rarely give it up. However, their Capricorn partner can make them question their convictions and feel lonely. If their Capricorn partner is too domineering, it can make Pisces lose their inspired and spontaneous nature.

Emotions

When these signs come together, they can build a deeply emotional bond over the years. They can bring out the best in each other and facilitate constant growth in their partner. They do this without making any major changes in their personality and just try to do the best they can in the relationship. While Pisces may seem unreliable and flaky, Capricorn can come across as grumpy. These signs can annoy each other if they remain too set in their opinions or views. When this happens, Pisces will disappoint their earthly Capricorn partner, and Capricorn will drain the magic out of Pisces.

Values

The way that these signs approach their values is consistent in a way. Surprisingly, Pisces value stable emotions when they are in a long-term relationship. Capricorn also places value on their partner's ability to be emotional and think positively. This goes against their very nature but is the way they approach their values in this relationship.

However, they have problems when they have to use these beliefs or emotions in their everyday life. Pisces will not be able to value the cool-headedness or rationality of Capricorn. Sometimes they can be too different since Capricorn thinks it is impossible to find the perfect love Pisces dreams of. It is not easy for either of them, but they can overcome these differences if they value each other enough.

Shared Activities

At the beginning of their relationship, both partners will spend all their time together. This is in spite of the fact that they usually have very different interests. Capricorn will want to enter the world of their Pisces partner, while Pisces will want to figure out the mind of their Capricorn partner. As they spend more time together, they will start taking part in different activities.

Pisces will realize that the interests of Capricorn are boring, at least to them. Capricorn will find the hobbies of Pisces crazy since they are not useful or well-planned. However, they will spend time doing some things together because they value traditions. While Pisces has a romantic idea about tradition, Capricorn respects tradition itself. Despite the different approaches, they will want to have some shared activities.

Capricorn and Pisces have a love story that is all about inspiration. Pisces is the one sign that can pull Capricorn into an exciting and unpredictable love story. Capricorn is the sign that can bring stability and peace into the emotional rollercoaster of a Pisces' life. Their relationship will make Capricorn more optimistic and cheerful, while Pisces can act more practically and think realistically. However, their love for Jupiter can cause some challenges. The different approaches that these signs have towards faith and religion can make it difficult for them to reconcile at times. This is why it is important that they each ask themselves if their own belief system works and if that of their partner does too. They just have to find a way to accept and respect each other's Jupiter.

I hope you can use this information to learn more about your partner or choose a partner from the sign that is most compatible with you. There are always exceptions to the rules, so you cannot judge a person just by their sign. However, certain relationships will have an easy flow to them, while others will require a lot more work. You also need to ensure that your partner is dedicated enough to the relationship to work through those obstacles that come when certain signs blend. But with a little time and sincerity, you can use this information to understand your partner further and improve your relationship.

Chapter Seven: Capricorn Friendships

This section will cover friendships, social life, and how the Capricorn functions in the world around them.

Capricorn takes their friendships seriously, just like everything else in their lives. They are loyal and loving, all about the shared stories and inside jokes. They like taking care of their friends and making them dinner. They use their strengths to help their friends as best as they can.

Capricorns encourage and motivate their friends and help bring out the best in them. They also aren't shy about letting their friends know when they are disappointed in them. They don't ignore bad behavior and call out a friend if they notice something they consider wrong. Capricorns are not the life of the party and like being in bed on time. They are not a fun friend, but they are always the ones with the best gifts. They are dedicated to their friends and expect the same.

How to be Friends with a Capricorn

To get close to a Capricorn, you have to be persistent. This sign may seem distant, but they just want to see if it is worth it before they invest in it. Capricorns are very observant and take time to judge if a person is worthy of being part of their inner circle. Capricorns value good character since they are very honest themselves.

To be friends with a Capricorn, you have to be loyal, hard-working, and honest. This is what will impress them. Also, display your skills to them since they are attracted to such things. To spend time with a Capricorn, choose a useful activity like a class where they can learn something, or join them for a walk or hike just for the health of it. A coffee date or dinner will seem pointless to them most of the time.

To maintain a good friendship with a Capricorn, you have to make an effort to stay in touch with them. Keep their birthdays and important events in mind. Check in with them regularly and send gifts once in a while. Capricorns don't like short-term friends who disappear from their lives. They appreciate the ones who stay or keep in touch even if it is a long-distance friendship.

Capricorns love to reminisce about the old days and talk about shared stories. They may not seem like a sentimental sort, but they really are. They like saving photos and looking at them once in a while. Keeping a framed picture of your Capricorn friend will show them that you treasure their friendship.

Capricorns Make Good Friends

They are Loyal

They do their best to have your back and protect you. Even if they don't agree with your choices, they will try to stand by you. They are somewhat parental in nature and give lectures, but it is only in your best interest.

They Remember Important Things

If you visit your Capricorn friend, they will make your favorite food or have your favorite wine ready. They will remember your tastes and give you exactly what you want for your birthday. They will remember the details of every story you tell them and the names of every ex or family member you talk about. This friend will know you inside out.

They Appreciate Your Strengths and Accept Your Flaws

Capricorns are usually like a guidance counselor for their friends. They will help you make plans and put your goals into action. They know what you are good at and how you can use it to your benefit. They will also know your weaknesses and accept you despite them.

Capricorn Friendships with the Other 11 Zodiac Signs

Capricorn and Aries

It can be challenging for Capricorn to have an Aries friend. Although Capricorn is up for the challenge, their opposite personality will clash. Aries is hotheaded while Capricorn is coolheaded. While Capricorn likes to savor their life, Aries likes rushing through it. Both are very ambitious and can have a strong bond if they support each other's ambitions.

Capricorn and Taurus

A Capricorn will always treasure their great friendship with a Taurus. This sign is humorous, loving, and loyal. They will admire the qualities of their Capricorn friend just as the sea-goat admires their virtues. Taurus will constantly praise the drive, dependability, and sophistication of a Capricorn. Both signs want financial stability so they can retire early. These friends love talking about their dreams for the future and what they want to do once they have achieved their goals. Any minor issues will barely affect their friendship over the years.

Capricorn and Gemini

Capricorn finds it hard to understand their Gemini friend, but it is not from lack of trying. The Gemini is an unpredictable bunch, and you can never tell for sure what makes them tick. They could be interested in one thing today and another tomorrow. Their rash behavior is difficult for practical Capricorn to bear. Gemini, on the other hand, finds the reluctance of Capricorn to try new things annoying. But Gemini friends are willing to put up with Capricorns if the latter learns to deal with their unpredictability.

Capricorn and Cancer

Although Cancer is the astrological opposite of Capricorn, they can still be friends. Cancer friends are compassionate and caring, and this can make Capricorns warm up to them. The executive ability of a Capricorn is similar to that of Cancer, and the latter considers them a kindred spirit. However, Cancer is a lot more emotional and sentimental than Capricorns. Nonetheless, these signs can create a good balance for each other.

Capricorn and Leo

Having these signs as friends will always attract attention. This could be positive or negative, depending on some factors. Leo is an outgoing friend who makes it easier for the introverted Capricorn to meet new people. But the sunny personality of Leo can outshine the quiet Capricorn. These two should avoid competing for the same things if they want to remain friends. Leo will be better friends with someone who is humorous, while Capricorn will resonate with people who have dry humor.

Capricorn and Virgo

The friendship between these two signs is quite noteworthy. Both signs are cautious, but they seem to take an instant liking to each other. Once they start talking, they realize that they both like activities like gardening. However, they could go about it differently. Virgo appreciates the slow pace at which Capricorn enjoys things while

Capricorn likes the modesty of a Virgo. These two will be friends forever if they can overlook each other's flaws.

Capricorn and Libra

The friendship between these two signs is only possible if both consciously overlook their differences. Libra is a very different sign from Capricorn, and it is usually difficult for them to get along. Capricorn is focused on facts while Libra plays with concepts. Capricorns are steady folks, while Libras are constantly changing.

Libra will find it difficult to understand Capricorn's serious nature while the latter will hate the inability of Libra to make decisions. The one thing these friends will have in common is their leadership ability. Capricorn is good at managing materials, while Libra is better at executing ideas. Combining both talents can be beneficial for these friends. When they work at building something together, it makes their friendship function well, too.

Capricorn and Scorpio

These signs find great comfort in their friendship. Scorpio will understand Capricorn's cautiousness, and the latter will sympathize with how Scorpio plays their cards close. This pair will be comfortable in their silences and don't mind that neither talks a lot. The only hitch is that Scorpio does not like bossy behavior, and Capricorn will be uncomfortable with the grudge-holding Scorpio. But for the most part, they are congenial together. These signs have similar humor and enjoy dark comedies.

Capricorn and Sagittarius

Capricorn admires the traits of Sagittarius like their humor and honesty. Sagittarius, on the other hand, admires the drive and determination of Capricorn. This is why these two signs will want to be friends with each other. Both will help each other out when needed.

Capricorn and Capricorn

Having a friend from the same zodiac sign can be nice for Capricorn. They know that their friend will never leave them hanging or act irresponsibly. They can depend on them to look after a pet when they are away or to stay by their side at a party. These friends don't like discussing their darkest secrets, but they can depend on each other when needed. Being similar, they know that they can trust each other to keep their secrets safe and to stay loyal.

Capricorn and Aquarius

The most obvious friend for Capricorn is not Aquarius, but it still works for this pair. The unpredictable behavior of Aquarius acts as a catharsis for Capricorn. This sign reminds Capricorn it helps to toss out the rules at times and follow your instinct. Capricorn teaches Aquarius friends the value of traditions. But Aquarius will usually accuse Capricorn of being boring and stuck up while the latter will tire of Aquarius's rebellious nature.

Capricorn and Pisces

Capricorn is always willing to act as a sanctuary for Pisces, who look for shelter in them. They know that Pisces will be there to comfort them in their time of need. While Capricorn is usually quite introverted, they openly shed their tears in front of their Pisces friend. However, the lack of punctuality in Pisces can be very annoying for the punctual Capricorn. But most of the time, these friends get along quite well.

Capricorn at a Party

It is rare to see Capricorns out on the town every day. However, they always show up to a party when it matters. If it is a birthday or an event for their closest friends or family, Capricorn will always make it. They never flake on such days even though they like being in bed early. Capricorns are also great at hosting a themed party for their friends once in a while.

If you invite your Capricorn friend to a holiday party, they will be there without fail. While this sign is not very extroverted, that is not the case when they are with their trusted ones. If they accompany a friend to a stranger's party, they act responsibly and stay with their friend all throughout. They will drink a few but never more than they can handle. If they know no one at a party, they will make polite conversation and try to leave when it is acceptable to do so. This sign may not be the life of the party, but they have fun in their own way with the people they genuinely like.

Chapter Eight: Capricorn at Work – Capricorn Career Paths

In this section, we will look at Capricorn at work. Certain types of professions are better suited for the personality of a Capricorn. They do better in their careers when they choose these. You will also learn about the compatibility of Capricorns with other signs at their workplace.

Best Career Choices For Capricorn

Capricorns are best suited for a career in which they are able to capitalize on the strengths associated with their zodiac sign. Capricorns are inherently hard working and love dedicating themselves to a particular task. A Capricorn has a strong suit for being organized and patient. They can follow routines well, and they have a strong work ethic which helps them to multitask and thrive in a corporate world. Considering these traits, here are some of the best-suited career options available for Capricorn men and women.

Teacher

Teaching requires you to have a lot of patience, along with strong organizational skills. This makes this particular career choice a good fit for Capricorns. Teachers need to be able to stay organized and be able to handle twenty or thirty students in a class setting.

Teachers also need to have a lot of patience for dealing with young children, who tend to have short attention spans. All these challenges make Capricorns a perfect fit for the teaching profession. However, also remember that many Capricorns cannot relate to young children. There are also plenty of Leos and Gemini in the teaching profession because of their rare ability to relate to other people, including young children.

Professional Manager/Organizer

A Capricorn's strong suit is for being organized and being able to handle different things simultaneously, making them great professional managers and organizers, and even home decorators; they can effectively help their clients organize their homes, commercial spaces, or offices.

Most people without a lot of the traits of the Earth sign in their personal horoscopes cannot lead organized lives, and they need a Capricorn's help to organize themselves. Organization is something that comes naturally to a Capricorn and capitalizing on it professionally can bring a lot of success.

Accounting/Financial Management

Accounting can be considered the perfect dream job for a Capricorn. Capricorns are excellent at managing finances. Their strong organizational skills help them prepare large financial statements, making them great at accounting and financial planning. They can carry out these tasks with ease and almost perfectly, with no mistakes. Accountancy and financial planning is not a job meant for everyone, and most people do not enjoy doing it, but for Capricorns, it is something that comes naturally to them.

Like an accountant, a financial planner's job also entails working with the same management of finances and numbers, bank statements, and fund investments that accounting requires. Capricorns are great at predicting when to move funds and finding better areas that yield higher profits. They are great at managing risks, and they can guide people and organizations to financial security. Capricorns are proficient at financial management; it's something that comes to them easily.

Business Executive

Most corporate heads and managers are Capricorns; this can be a tough role to fulfill for most people since it requires strong organizational skills and excellent problem-solving capabilities. Being an executive also requires a lot of patience for dealing with many different types of people. It is also the manager's job to decide who deserves a raise or a promotion depending upon their performance, and Capricorns are great at making decisions by detaching themselves from these situations emotionally.

Programming and Information Technology

Being a skilled computer programmer requires exceptional problem solving and organizational skills. Capricorns are naturals when it comes to computer programming, coding, and data management. Although most people may find this job to be boring, Capricorns are tenacious and can focus on problems and work at it until they come up with a solution.

Capricorn Work Compatibility

Capricorns are one of the most persevering zodiac signs. If you are a Capricorn, the chances are good that you leave your employers feeling impressed with your drive, determination, and practical solutions. While other zodiac signs such as Sagittarius and Libra are adept at handling the social aspects of being in a workplace, Capricorns have a different disposition and prefer keeping a low profile and focusing on doing their best work.

Capricorn and Aries

While Capricorn is able to admire and relate to The Ram's high energy and strong work ethic, there can be some friction due to their brash behavior. As a Capricorn, you are the type of person who prefers to cover your strong and independent core with a soft and approachable velvet cover. Aries tend to overlook these niceties, and their brash behavior may not sit well with you.

While their brutish behavior may make you wince, you cannot deny that they can achieve a lot and bring some great results. Instead of criticizing them for their shortcomings, try to channel their talents to help you in different situations. After all, there is no point in issuing futile rebukes to people who are set in their ways and unwilling to back down. Similarly, it is also best to be direct and question them if you feel like something doesn't sit well with you.

While an Aries can help you with handling the aggressive aspects of your business, you can take charge of the duties that require finesse and subtlety. Together, you can make a great duo and do some significant work in your own unique ways.

Capricorn and Taurus

A Taurus can make a wonderful colleague for Capricorns, mainly because they share the same core values. Both Capricorns and Taurus seek jobs that offer stability, profitability, and luxury. If a Capricorn and a Taurus decide to go into business together, they can use their unique skills to create and sustain profitable ventures such as five-star restaurants, luxury car dealerships, and other high-end businesses. A Capricorn and a Taurus can quickly rise up through the ranks by providing each other valuable help and support.

By being the person who sets a higher standard for this modest zodiac sign, you can help them unlock their full potential, and they will reward you with their undying loyalty. A Taurus is also great at reining you in when you're going too hard and are at the risk of burning out. You need a reminder sometimes to take a break so that you can do your best work.

Capricorn and Gemini

Geminis are not the easiest people to work with if you are a Capricorn. That does not mean that the two cannot coexist together peacefully. The important thing to remember is that Geminis are not the best at following a routine regularly. Therefore you need to be a little smart while assigning tasks to a Gemini. Assign them with fast-paced responsibilities such as handling the reception desk, answering phones, taking orders, and waiting on customers while you are focusing on the long-term goals such as making financial projections, meeting deadlines, and formulating marketing strategies.

Although a Gemini may seem flaky to you, you cannot deny that a Gemini's optimistic attitude can brighten the atmosphere and bring out the best in you as well. Try not to be too reprimanding because of their eager behavior; after all, they have only your best interests at heart. The two of you can create a very dynamic duo and make successful curators, auctioneers, and archivists.

Capricorn and Cancer

Although the Crab is your astrological opposite, the two of you can work very efficiently as a professional team. Most Capricorns are workaholics, and they need someone who can identify that and tell them to slow them down and take it easy to avoid burning out. Cancer is perfect for this job. Similarly, a sensitive zodiac sign like the Crab needs a lot of praise and encouragement for them to function at their best, which a Capricorn can provide in spades.

Yes, your colleague's sensitive and moody nature can get on your nerves at certain times, but your professional side and no-nonsense nature can cut a Cancer to the core. If you are able to overcome these differences and admire each other's strengths, you can be an effective and efficient duo. Both of you are blessed with leadership qualities, although a Cancer is more gifted at working with different kinds of people while a Capricorn is better suited for working with products.

If you are planning to enter into a business partnership with a Cancer, consider going into the investment banking sector or the shipping industry.

Capricorn and Leo

Leos can make stimulating but challenging colleagues for Capricorns. Both of you are capable of tremendous hard work and have strong work ethics, although you may hold very different needs and goals. The Lion seeks fame while a Capricorn's main goal is a fortune. Leos loves leading a glamorous lifestyle while a Capricorn enjoys understated elegance.

Leos are notorious for spending lavishly on their indulgences while a Capricorn saves obsessively. However, if you can manage to overcome these differences, the two of you can create a powerful partnership and build a profitable empire. You will find a lot of success in real estate and other marketing agencies. A Leo loves working with people and being in the limelight. while you can keep busy behind the scenes orchestrating the operation and making the important decisions. A Capricorn is good at handling finances, but it may serve you well to listen to a Leo and work on your presentation.

Capricorn and Virgo

Working with a Virgo is akin to having your prayers answered. You can never find a more hard-working and honest colleague. A Virgo will never stand in your way professionally, and they will actually try to make your journey a smoother one.

If you are patient with a Virgo and make your expectations clear, you will receive nothing less than a stellar performance from this zodiac sign. Be mindful and remember that this is one of the star signs that are extremely prone to stress and burning out due to stress. If you are working alongside a Virgo, you are better off letting your colleague handle the day-to-day operations while you focus on the long-term projects and the bigger picture. Together, the two of you can use your combined skill sets to get the best results.

Capricorn and Libra

As a Capricorn, you appreciate and admire professionalism, and Libras certainly make a good show of the fine work that they do. Yes, their attitude may seem shallow and frivolous at times, but that may only be prejudice as the result of your own serious approach to doing things.

The two of you will need to meet each other halfway and find a middle ground that will work for both of you. You cannot deny that this zodiac sign has a very intelligent head on their shoulders. They have very strong powers of analysis and are keen on learning new things. At the same time, you are an expert at spinning straw into gold and creating something out of nothing.

This is something that a Libra will very much appreciate and admire. If you are working with a Libra, let them be the face of the operation and handle the clientele while you handle the executive operations. Although both of you may be blessed with strong executive abilities, you are much better at making decisions for the long run.

Capricorn and Scorpio

A Scorpio and a Capricorn make a very productive duo since both are extremely hardworking. This is also because a Scorpio has no problem with you being at the helm of the operation. In fact, Scorpios prefer working behind the scenes while gathering an intellectual edge over competitors. While a Scorpio keeps busy building financial dossiers, you can be the face of the operation and impress your clientele with your professionalism, diligence, and hard work.

You can rely on the Scorpion when it comes to facts and figures, which can then be incorporated into reports and presentations to impress your clientele. Although you may have small spats and gripes with each other, there is nothing that the two of you can't work your way around and create a powerful and productive partnership professionally.

Capricorn and Sagittarius

A Sagittarius' laid-back attitude can prove to be a distraction for you sometimes since you are an extremely professional and goal-oriented person. Although a Capricorn and Sagittarius have very conflicting traits, the truth is that a Sagittarius can be extremely important for the sake of your success.

This zodiac sign can connect with people from different walks of life, and the two of you can create a very diverse and impressive clientele and carve out a unique niche for yourselves. Besides that, a Sagittarius is also extremely honest and will likely keep a check on you to avoid any bad decisions being made. Similarly, you can also lend a much-needed structure and regimen to a Sagittarius' laid-back nature to bring out the best in them.

Capricorn and Aquarius

An Aquarius may attempt to test your patience during certain situations, but that does not mean that it is impossible for the two of you to co-exist and work in a partnership. Although this zodiac sign is more known for its creativity, you cannot deny its strong problem-solving skills. Similarly, an Aquarius will admire your strong work ethic and your ability to tackle big responsibilities without even letting out a hint of a complaint.

Capricorn and Capricorn

You will enjoy – and benefit from – working with a fellow Capricorn; they are known to be dedicated, tenacious, and capable. If times are lean, you can be confident that your mutual resourcefulness will help you both endure this period. While you may both be susceptible to the monotony of tough times (sticking to the plan), your dry sense of humor helps get you through those days. Your work together will build solid and enduring structures born of critical thinking and dignity. Together, you'll find great success as investment bankers, real estate developers, or architects. Consider opening a dentistry practice; you'll surely find success in that endeavor, as well!

Capricorn and Pisces

Your Pisces workmate brings a whimsical lightness to the business setting, despite your no-nonsense approach. Interoffice memos become an opportunity for levity, and your office phone's ringtones are programmed in swing tunes or upbeat tones! With any other astrologically-signed cohort, this might drive you mad; with a Pisces, you find yourself playing along and enjoying the fun. This Fish "gets" you like no one else in this office, never considering your ambition as greed or your professional demeanor as stuffy or tedious. Under your direction, you'll find that Pisces take their creative ideas and turn them into profitable products and services. At the same time, the Fish's creative influence behaves as fuel for your own imagination. Together, you two could manage a successful film studio, shipping line, or medical practice.

Work is one aspect of their life that Capricorns will always do well in as long as they love what they do.

Chapter Nine: What Does a Capricorn Need?

By now, you know a lot about the distinctive traits of Capricorn and what makes them different from other zodiac signs. For a Capricorn to succeed in their life, they have to remember some things.

An individual from this zodiac sign should be more confident about their decisions, whether at work or at home. Especially at the workplace, they have to learn to value their own decisions and thus gain respect from their colleagues at work.

While at work, this sign should work at looking more interested in their work. It is often seen that they are in a rush to leave when they get their work done even if colleagues are still at their desks. Changing this habit can be helpful and will make people notice their dedication.

Capricorns should try to choose things they love or are well suited for them instead of following the crowd. While they like the comfort and security in following others, they could achieve a lot more success if they walk the path less taken.

It is better for a Capricorn not to work with their spouse or even at the same place as them. This sign is very competitive and controlling, so this can have a negative impact on their relationship. Having a separate workplace is highly recommended for Capricorns and their partners. This would allow them to have space for their personal growth without being influenced by each other.

Capricorns need to try something new sometimes. This will help them gain exposure, come out of their comfort zone, and become worldly.

The individuals from this sign also need to work on becoming better listeners. While they have strong opinions and like expressing themselves, they should also give others the chance to do so. Letting someone talk without interrupting is a skill this sign needs to acquire. It will help them learn from the people around them and make them better listeners.

Having some "me" time every day can also be beneficial for their wellbeing. It will help them feel better and have more control over their temper even on the worst of days.

Being realistic is an inborn characteristic of Capricorn. However, it is also important for them to learn to be more positive in life. It is okay to hope for the best, even if you feel like there is a chance for things to go wrong. Indulging in some flighty dreams at times can be good for them.

Capricorns also needs to stop criticizing themselves all the time. They should think about the things they tell themselves and decide if it were something they would ever tell someone they loved. Constant self-criticism will only bring down their self-confidence and affect their abilities.

These things are some simple points that a Capricorn should keep in mind.

Conclusion

By now, you know a lot about a Capricorn's personality, along with their strengths and weaknesses. You also know how their mind works most of the time, and this can help you understand this standoffish sign better.

For a Capricorn, it is crucial to find the right partner in love who will help balance out their weaknesses and bring out the best in them. It is also important for them to be with a person who will understand their need to work hard and take their time as they go about things.

Many things are unique and admirable about this zodiac sign. I hope you found the information in this book about Capricorn enlightening. You can even recommend it to other Capricorns or people with Capricorns in their lives.

Here's another book by Mari Silva that you might like

THE ULTIMATE GUIDE TO AN AMAZING
ZODIAC SIGN IN ASTROLOGY

PISCES

MARI SILVA

Your Free Gift (only available for a limited time)

Thanks for getting this book! If you want to learn more about various spirituality topics, then join Mari Silva's community and get a free guided meditation MP3 for awakening your third eye. This guided meditation mp3 is designed to open and strengthen ones third eye so you can experience a higher state of consciousness. Simply visit the link below the image to get started.

https://spiritualityspot.com/meditation

References

Capricorn Child: Capricorn Girl & Boy Traits & Personality | Zodiac Signs for Kids. (n.d.). www.buildingbeautifulsouls.com website: https://www.buildingbeautifulsouls.com/zodiac-signs/zodiac-signs-kids/capricorn-child-traits-characteristics-personality/

Capricorn Traits-Positive and Negative Characteristics | Ganeshaspeaks.com. (2016, November 29). GaneshaSpeaks website: https://www.ganeshaspeaks.com/zodiac-signs/capricorn/traits/

Faragher, A. K. (2020, July 31). Here's What the Capricorn Personality Is Really Like. Allure website: https://www.allure.com/story/capricorn-zodiac-sign-personality-traits

My Capricorn Zodiac Sign: Friendship. (n.d.). www.horoscope.com website: https://www.horoscope.com/zodiac-signs/capricorn/friendship

Thinnes, C. (2020, February 17). Capricorn Compatibility - Best and Worst Matches. Numerologysign.com website: https://numerologysign.com/astrology/zodiac/compatibility/capricorn-compatibility/

Tips on how Capricorns get to be even more awesome at life. (n.d.). www.horoscope.com website: https://www.horoscope.com/us/editorial/editorial-news.aspx?UniqueID=3310&CRC=295F9C29D08F59DE69C1D56A092D0DCF

Printed in Great Britain
by Amazon